Dictionary of Vitamins and Essential Minerals

BROCKHAMPTON PRESS
LONDON

This edition published 1996 by Brockhampton Press, a member of Hodder Headline PLC.

ISBN 1 86019 340 4

Printed and bound in India

Contents

Introduction

Human health is governed by two critical factors—the inherited genetic characteristics from our parents and our environment and living habits. We can do nothing to alter our genetic inheritance, but we can benefit our health by choosing the correct lifestyle and living habits. This should mean we lower our risks of developing certain diseases, e.g. cancer, and extend our life-span and improve our quality of life.

Our health can be influenced by a huge range of factors—eating habits, alcohol, exercise, coffee, occupation, food quality, tobacco, sleep and stress. This list is not a complete one, but it can be seen how many factors relate to the food and drink we consume. Much of the food eaten today is in a processed form, which is convenient but may be lacking in essential nutrients, vitamins and minerals. In a healthy diet, we should consume a balance of carbohydrates, proteins, fats, fibre, vegetables and fruit. Carbohydrates are starches and sugars found in foodstuffs, and they are the body's main source of energy. Health authorities recommend that we eat more starchy food, such as potatoes, bread, rice, pasta and maize, and cut down our intake of sugars, particularly refined sugars found in cakes, biscuits, chocolate, etc. Sugars do occur naturally in foods like milk and fruit but refined sugar has no nutrient value, it just has 'empty' calories. Proteins are required for the growth and repair of our body cells. Once digested, proteins break down into amino acids, which go to form new protein components inside cells. Humans need eight essential amino acids from proteins in our diet as they cannot be made inside our bodies. They include valine, leucine, methionine and tryptophan, the last of which can be converted into vitamin B_3 (niacin) in humans. Protein can be plant or animal in origin, but some of the plant protein sources may lack some of the essential amino acids. Protein is found in meat, fish, eggs, dairy products, whole-grain cereals, pasta, beans, maize, peas and nuts.

We also need fats in our diet. When digested, fats release fatty acids, which are needed to build and repair cells and to act as chemical messengers to activate body functions. Fat is also used as an energy source. There are two types of fat: saturated and unsaturated. Saturated fats are hard at room temperature as they have a structure with as many hydrogen atoms as possible in it (hence saturated fat). They are found in dairy foods, beef, lamb, pork, meat products, milk, eggs, cakes, biscuits, chocolate and some vegetable oils, e.g. coconut and palm oil. Saturated fats in our diet may be used to produce cholesterol in the liver. Many people have heard of cholesterol as it may be linked to heart attacks or stroke. Cholesterol is essential for many body functions, including making hormones and reproduction.

There are two forms of cholesterol: low-density lipoprotein (LDL) and high density lipoprotein (HDL). LDL-cholesterol is the 'bad' form of the fat as it removes some LDL-cholesterol to the cells for use but leaves any excess in the bloodstream where it can gradually block the arteries, reducing blood flow and increasing the risks of heart attack or strokes. HDL-cholesterol acts to remove this excess fat from the bloodstream and so reduces the chances of blocked arteries and circulatory problems.

Unsaturated fats are fats that do not have their full complement of hydrogen atoms in their structure. There are two types: polyunsaturated fats, which are found in fish, chicken, soft margarines labelled high in polyunsaturates, and very low fat spreads made with unsaturated oils. They are also found in vegetable oils like safflower, corn or sunflower oil and soya bean oil. Until recently, polyunsaturated fats were considered good for us and not damaging in the same way as saturated fats are. Now it appears that polyunsaturated fats are attacked by oxygen-free radicals, making them oxidized and rancid. This could lead to damage to the artery walls in our body. Instead, consumption of monounsaturated fats is encouraged. These are found in olive oil, rape-seed oil, peanut oil, peanuts, avocado and olives. There are also several monounsaturated fat spreads on the market, but care has to be taken as they may have been hardened into a solid by the addition of hydrogenated oil. This oil contains trans-fatty acids, which act similarly to saturated fats in our bloodstream. We should avoid spreads containing these fatty acids and some spreads now promote the reduced levels of trans-fatty acids in their product. Hydrogenated vegetable fat and oil is also found in biscuits, crisps, cakes and cereals.

Our diet should contain a good balance of carbohydrate, protein, vegetables, fruit, fibre and fats. A diet with not more than 30 per cent fat is recommended, with only a third of that saturated fat. We should eat more monounsaturated than polyunsaturated fats as well. This would decrease the levels of triglyceride fats in our blood (which come from our diet) and so reduce the risks of death from heart disease, particularly in women.

Fibre is the part of vegetable, fruits and unrefined cereal grains that we cannot digest. Like fats, there are two types, soluble and insoluble. Soluble fibre is found in fruit, vegetables, beans and oats, and in the body it modifies the absorption of fats and lowers the levels of blood cholesterol. Insoluble fibre acts to add bulk to the faeces, so helping its movement through the intestines and preventing constipation. It speeds up the time taken for digested food to move through the large intestine, so reducing exposure of the intestine to any harmful toxins or carcinogens present in our food. This is thought to help protect against cancer of the colon. Fibre can also stabilize sugar absorption, which is important for diabetics. Dietary fibre, however, may absorb some medicines and reduce their speed of absorption into the body. We should aim to eat 25g (1oz) of fibre every day.

Government health authorities now recommend we eat at least five portions of fruit and vegetables a day. Many of the chemicals that give the fruit or vegetables their colour are protective factors, and they work with vitamins in our food to stimulate the immune system. These protective factors are found in a massive range of fruit and vegetables, including cabbage, broccoli, carrots, strawberries, turnips, cauliflower, onions, green peppers, pineapples and tomatoes.

Another common item in our diet about which there is great debate is coffee. Conflicting studies have shown both protective and harmful effects from drinking coffee. The caffeine can overstimulate some people, causing agitation. Caffeine can also be addictive, even if drunk at only moderate levels. A study where people who drank 2–3 cups of coffee a day stopped doing so resulted in some people having headaches, anxiety and depression. It is probably wise to cut down on the levels of caffeine taken in drinks or to replace it with coffee substitutes or herbal teas, which do not contain caffeine. Tea also contains caffeine, so its intake should be limited as well.

The vegetarian diet

A vegetarian diet requires the same balance of carbohydrate, protein, fats, fibre but with a higher emphasis on vegetables and fruit. The degree to which a diet is vegetarian varies, as some people exclude meat, poultry and fish but others do leave fish in their diets. A lacto-vegetarian excludes eggs but eats milk and milk products, while an ovo-vegetarian eats both eggs and milk products. This is along with the normal vegetarian diet of vegetables, fruit, beans, grains, nuts, sprouts and mushrooms. A vegan does not eat any product from the animal kingdom. The risk of malnutrition and vitamin or mineral deficiency is not as great as once thought with a vegetarian diet. Adequate levels of essential amino acids can be obtained from plant proteins, eggs, milk and from pulses. Vitamins such as cyanocobalamin (B_{12}) are not present in plants, so a vegan may become deficient in this nutrient. Vitamin B_{12} is present in milk, so lacto- or ovo-vegetarians are not at risk from lack of vitamins B_{12}, D or B_2 (riboflavin). Vitamin-fortified soya milk contains vitamins D, B_{12} and B_2, but since this is not consumed by vegans they may require supplements. Calcium may also be lacking in vegans although it is present in tofu, flour, corn meal, sesame seeds, molasses and almond or filbert nuts. Vegetarians are commonly thought to be anaemic and lacking in iron as the best source of iron is meat. Iron from vegetables is harder to absorb into the body, but this can be helped by eating vitamin C-rich fruits, which aid absorption of iron.

Soya beans or their products, e.g. milk, tofu, often replace eggs, milk and meat in vegetarian diets, and they contain protein, vitamin E, iron, calcium, magnesium and phosphorus. Vegetarians need to have a balanced diet. If not they may develop deficiencies of selenium, copper, zinc, magnesium and lack sufficient dietary fibre. Children are at particular risk of too little vitamin D and calcium if they have a vegetarian diet. Women should take supplements of vitamin B_{12} as deficiency can cause irreversible nerve and brain damage. This is a particular risk when a woman is pregnant or breastfeeding, as the infant can deplete her stores of B_{12} and the child can suffer damage too if B_{12} is lacking. All vegan mothers are recommended to eat products fortified with vitamin B_{12} or to take B_{12} supplements.

The digestive process

The human digestive system is made up of the alimentary canal and several glands that secrete digestive juices into it. Food enters the mouth and is chewed so the teeth break down the food, increasing its surface area and making it easier to swallow. Saliva is produced from the salivary glands, and this lubricates the food and delivers a digestive enzyme to the mouth. This enzyme, called salivary amylase, breaks down starch into a smaller sugar called maltose. Saliva also helps to neutralize acid in the mouth and kill most of the bacteria present in the oral cavity. The food is swallowed and 5–10 seconds later it has moved down the oesophagus and entered the stomach. This organ is large enough to store a whole meal, so humans do not have to eat constantly in the same way as some animals do. The stomach lining produces gastric juice, which has an acidic pH of around 2. This acid kills any bacteria swallowed with the food and helps to break down the intercellular connections in meat or plants. An enzyme called pepsin is also found in gastric juice, and it breaks down proteins into smaller polypeptide units.

The contents of the stomach are mixed by the churning action of the muscles, and a nutrient mixture called acid chyme is produced. Despite public belief, little digestion of the food occurs in the stomach. Over a period of two to six hours after a meal, the acid chyme is released into the small intestine. Here digestive juices from the intestinal wall, pancreas, liver and gall bladder are mixed with the chyme. Bile is produced from the gall bladder, and it acts to help in the digestion and absorption of fats because of the bile salts it contains. Maltose is broken down into glucose by an enzyme called maltose, and milk sugar (lactose) and sucrose are broken down by similar enzymes. The sugars are then absorbed through the intestinal wall into the bloodstream.

Protein digestion works by using several enzymes as a team. Enzymes called trypsin and chemotrypsin break the proteins into smaller lengths, and then carboxypeptidase and aminopeptidase start removing one amino acid at a time from opposite ends of the protein molecules. This teamwork allows for faster hydrolysis of the proteins. The DNA and RNA present in food are digested in a similar team mechanism by nuclease enzymes. Very little of the fat content in a meal is digested before it reaches the small intestine. Bile salts coat droplets of fats and emulsify them so there is a large surface area for the lipase enzyme to attack. This produces glycerides, fatty acids and glycerol. All these digestive products are absorbed in the lower sections of the small intestine. These sections have a very large surface area over which the nutrients can diffuse into the blood and lymph fluids. Some sugars, e.g. fructose, diffuses across the epithelium while amino acids, glucose, vitamins and other sugars have to be pumped across the membranes. The glycerol and fatty acids recombine to form fats, and these may bind to special proteins to form lipoproteins, e.g. cholesterol. Amino acids, nucleotides and sugars travel to the liver, and from there to the heart and the rest of the body. Water in the diet is re-absorbed through the large intestine, and any undigested material is moved down the intestine to the rectum. Faeces are stored there until they are eliminated. Some beneficial bacteria live in the large intestine, including those that produce vitamin K. Most of our daily needs of this vitamin can be met by the production of these bacteria.

The nutritional benefits derived from food can be lost if there is a disorder of the stomach, liver, intestines or any of the associated enzyme-producing glands. Absorption of some vitamins and minerals is affected by disorders of the liver, pancreas or gall bladder, and also by the presence of dietary fibre or other vitamins and minerals. Copper and zinc compete to be absorbed into the body, while absorption of calcium is affected by the presence of vitamin D, stomach acids, fibre and the intake of proteins.

Interaction of medicine and nutrient absorption

Throughout the industrialized world medicines are extensively used to treat disease. Each person in Europe receives an average of five prescriptions each year. Many medicines are prescribed for more minor problems, and this may be because of pressure on the doctor rather than the necessity of the drugs for a cure to be obtained. Nearly half of all prescriptions are not used, and many of those utilized are not taken according to the doctor's instructions. Medicines affect the uptake of nutrients, vitamins and minerals into the body. Conversely, food can affect the absorption and effectiveness of many drugs. Some drugs should be taken on an empty stomach or before food so that they are rapidly digested and enter the bloodstream. Most medicines are best taken along with a meal, but this can delay absorption of the drug by two to five hours. All medicines are absorbed in the small intestine, where they compete for absorption with sugars, amino acids, nucleotides, vitamins, minerals and fats. Potassium can restrict uptake of the heart drug digoxin, while calcium, iron, zinc and magnesium form organic metal compounds with the common antibiotic tetracycline so it is not properly absorbed.

Dietary fibre can absorb a proportion of medications so that it is removed from the body instead of entering the bloodstream. Certain medicines promote the formation of oxygen-free radicals, which are discussed later (see following section, 'Dangers to our cells'). Prescribed medicines should be used carefully as some can affect the appetite and lead to nutritional problems while others, e.g. diuretic drugs, can lead to the excess elimination of some minerals, e.g. potassium and magnesium, and possible deficiency.

Dangers to our cells

Each and every one of our cells has a specific life-span, which can range from approximately 110 to 120 years for brain cells to several days for some cell types. Not all cells last to their full potential as many substances can damage them and their processes. This cell death or damage gradually builds up over time, leading to illness that may reduce our life-span. Four main processes cause damage to cells:

—oxygen-free radicals
—lipid peroxidation
—degradation of the protein molecules
—cell changes or mutations

These changes are derived from our environment and lifestyle, not our genetic inheritance.

Free radicals are chemicals that have one or more unpaired electrons in their outer shell. They are therefore highly reactive. Free radicals are produced naturally in humans as they are vital for normal functioning of the body, but they can also be generated by certain drugs and by a process called reperfusion injury. Free radicals in humans are mainly oxygen-free radicals, which can form compounds that damage our health. The most common oxygen-free radicals are superoxide (O_2^-), hydrogen peroxide (H_2O_2), hydroxyl radical (OH^-) and singlet oxygen. When produced, they exist for a very short time, possibly only a fraction of a second. Despite their short duration, they still attack the cell structure and cause damage. They attack the fatty acids that make up the membranes of all cells and oxidize them. This makes the fats rancid and damages the membrane structure of the cell. The lipids in the membrane are changed into lipid peroxides, which allow the formation of new free radicals. This chain reaction, where free radicals are regenerated, eventually leads to the destruction of the cell. Lipid peroxides can be released into the bloodstream, e.g. oxidized LDL-cholesterol, which causes irritation of the artery walls and increases the risk of arteriosclerosis. These chemicals also inhibit the formation of PGI2, prostacyclin, a prostaglandin that stops blood clots forming in the blood vessels. The oxidized fats in the membrane can degrade to form harmful prostaglandins and a toxic chemical called malonaldehyde, which can cause mutations in the genetic material of cells.

Free radicals can damage the connective tissue. Collagen makes up 30 per cent of our body's protein, and it is found in the muscles, sinews, bones and cartilage, compared to elastin, which is a connective tissue found in the skin, the artery walls and the walls of the air sacs in the lungs. Free radicals cause cross-linkages between the collagen and elastin fibres, so reducing their ability to move, stretch and bend. This means the skin and other connective tissues go hard and stiff and age quickly. Cross-linkages can lead to modifications of the blood vessels and arteriosclerosis. Action of the free radicals may cause increased levels of ageing pigments, e.g. melamine, ceroid and lipofuscin, to develop in the nerves, internal organs, the skin and the grey matter of the brain. Free radicals may also oxidize and destroy large carbohydrate molecules, which would normally be used to form mucous. Mucous acts as a joint lubricant, so free radicals can lead to joint problems.

People who are overweight have higher levels of oxidized fats in their bodies and so a greater risk of heart infarction and arteriosclerosis. Animal experiments in which the calorific intake of the animals was restricted showed an increased life-span. When this was combined with the addition of antioxidants to their diet it prevented the formation of cancer. This is because antioxidants work to protect our bodies against free radicals, lipid peroxidation, harmful chemicals, and even cancer. Natural antioxidants in our diet include vitamins A, C and E, beta-carotene, zinc and selenium. Many chronic and long-term illnesses are thought to be associated with the destructive actions of free radicals. During a heart attack the blood flow in the coronary arteries is constricted, and the area is deprived of oxygen. When normal blood flow resumes, large quantities of oxygen-free radicals are formed, and these attack the damaged cells of the heart. They oxidize some of the cellular lipids and increase the chances of another heart attack or of cardiac arrhythmia developing. Cataracts would appear to develop because of free radicals. There are normally large quantities of natural antioxidants in the eye as the retinal cells are vulnerable to attack by free radicals. A malfunction in the oxygen metabolism, caused by light and free radicals, is commonly believed to cause cataracts. Eye problems can develop in babies kept in incubators. If the oxygen dose is not monitored closely, then oxygen radicals can damage the eye. The eyesight can be protected, thankfully, by supplements of vitamin E, which removes the free radicals.

The brain is also at risk from free radicals, as it contains a lot of unsaturated fatty acids, e.g. lecithin. If these lipids are oxidized, increased amounts of lipofuscin appear in the brain. Lipofuscin is one of the ageing pigments, which, when present in large quantities, speeds up the ageing process so the person becomes prematurely senile. In Alzheimer's disease, a specific group of brain cells develops a dark brown coloration as a result of oxidized fat in the cell structure. The production of free radicals is promoted by exposure to sunlight, environmental pollutants, ozone, X-rays, and cigarette smoke. A large range of medicines can also lead to more free radicals being formed. These include antibiotics, paracetamol, anti-epileptic medicines, cytotoxic drugs, theophyllin (for asthma), the antibiotic nitrofurantoin, which is used to treat urinary tract infections, and some psychopharmaceutical drugs. The list of diseases that are believed to be caused or exacerbated by free radicals increases all the time as the results of more clinical studies are obtained. Some examples are:

alcoholic liver/heart conditions	arthritis
auto-immune diseases	arteriosclerosis
circulation disturbances	cancer
coronary heart disease	cataract
emphysema of the lung	diabetes
inflammatory reactions	liver cirrhosis
multiple sclerosis (MS)	malaria
neuronal lipofuscinosis	porphyria
premature ageing	Parkinson's disease
retinal diseases	senile dementia]
rheumatoid diseases	side effects of medicines

Fortunately, we have a range of natural antioxidants that can defend our cells from free radicals and their harmful effects.

The antioxidant system

In the human body, vitamins, minerals, amino acids and specific enzymes work in cooperation to form the antioxidant system. These chemicals react with and neutralize free radicals, and they break the circle whereby free radicals degrade fatty acids and proteins, leading to the production of more free radicals and eventually causing the death of the cells. Effective antioxidants are selenium, zinc, manganese, copper, ubiquinone (co-enzyme Q10), vitamins A, C, E, B_1 (thiamine), B_3 (niacin), B_6 (pyroxidine) and possibly rutin, one of the group of bioflavonoids. Folic acid (vitamin B_9) and chemicals found in garlic and onions also have antioxidant qualities. Some amino acids, beta-carotene and some medicines also work as antioxidants. We obtain antioxidants from various sources, including tinned and processed foodstuffs. Antioxidants are added to food to prevent them from going rancid and to increase their shelf life, and this process has increased the average amount of antioxidants in our diets and reduced the incidence of diseases such as cancer or heart disease. Unfortunately, most people do not receive a high enough level of antioxidants in their normal diet to protect their health fully. Supplements of a combination of antioxidants can help protect all our cells from cancer, premature ageing and heavy metals, and aid the immune system.

The most important cells are those of the brain. Twenty per cent of the brain by weight is made up of polyunsaturated fatty acids, which are especially vulnerable to turning rancid. Recent evidence has shown that the ageing process in the brain is caused by these fatty acids being oxidized by free radicals. Most of the nervous system is also at risk, as nerve endings and the sheath around the nerves are composed of fatty material. The rancid fat is called lipofuscin, melamine and ceroid, or age pigments. If the nerve endings are oxidized, the senses of touch, smell, hearing, sight and taste can be affected. So nature has seen to it that the most vital cells in our brain are protected by large quantities of antioxidants. The spinal fluid that bathes the brain has a vitamin C content ten times that of the blood. In brain cells, vitamin C levels are 100 times that of the blood. The lens of the eye is also protected by high levels of vitamin C. So vitamin C is stored in areas where its antioxidant effects are most needed. Results from a series of controlled clinical studies showed that selenium, vitamin E, zinc and other antioxidants were effective in delaying the onset of degenerative diseases and stopping premature ageing.

Antioxidants such as zinc, vitamin E and selenium act against toxic heavy metals like cadmium, lead, mercury and aluminium. They reduce the level of damage done to the tissues by these elements. Selenium reacts with mercury so it cannot harm our cells. Selenium and vitamin E can reduce the unpleasant side effects of cytotoxic drugs, which are used during chemotherapy, for example.

Most minerals, vitamins, amino acids and essential fatty acids all play a very important role in the immune system.

The immune system

The immune system is made up of four major parts:

(a) cell-mediated immune response;
(b) humoral (antibody-mediated) immune response;
(c) white blood cells;
(d) complement system.

The first part of our defence against pathogens is the skin, mucous membranes and their secretions. If intact, this stops most bacteria and viruses from entering the body. If entry does occur, then the inflammatory response with its phagocytic white blood cells and antimicrobial proteins kick-starts. These antimicrobial proteins are the complement system and interferons. Complement is a group of over 20 proteins that can cause lysis of invading microbes as well as acting as chemical messengers for the white blood cells. Interferons are produced by a pathogen-infected cell and alert the neighbouring cells so they cannot become infected. It reduces the spread of infection and can also activate the phagocytes and improve their function. The inflammatory response produces increased heat and blood flow to the affected area with swelling. Chemical signals such as histamine or prostaglandins are released, and they have several actions. Phagocytes such as neutrophils and macrophages arrive at the injury, and they kill any pathogens by ingesting them and destroying them with enzymes. They also ingest debris of the cells that were damaged. Inflammatory reactions can be localized or found throughout the system. In some cases, molecules called pyrogens are released from white blood cells, and these trigger a fever to try and help the body fight the pathogen. These immune responses are nonspecific, and they occur in response to bacteria, viruses or physical injury in exactly the same manner.

The white blood cells are heavily involved in the specific immune response. There are five major types of white cells. Monocytes and neutrophils are phagocytic cells involved in the inflammatory response. Monocytes can develop into macrophages, which have an important role in cellular immunity. Basophils and eosinophils also work in the inflammatory reaction, while lymphocytes are the cells that produce antibodies or attack and kill pathogens.

The specific immune responses are derived from the humoral (antibody-mediated) or the cell-mediated response systems. Both B- and T-cells develop from stem cells in the bone marrow. When pathogens enter the body, they are termed 'antigen' (antibody-generating). Antigens include viruses, bacteria, protozoans, fungi and parasitic worms. When an antigen is encountered in the body, it generally meets one of the white blood cells, or leucocytes. The antigen may be taken up by a macrophage, which then changes into an antigen-presenting cell to warn other sections of the immune system of the invader.

A helper T-cell is triggered by this antigen-presenting cell, and it acts in two ways. It stimulates the humoral immune response to produce B-lymphocytes, which are made in the bone marrow. The B-cells produce two cell types—plasma cells and memory B-cells—both of which are specific to the original antigen. The plasma cells go on to make antibodies, which are specific to the pathogen, and they are released into the blood and lymph fluid to locate and bind to their specific antigenic pathogen. The memory B-cells survive in the body fluids for long periods and are reactivated, if and when they encounter the original antigen again, to provide a rapid response by producing antibodies and more memory cells. The memory cells allow a faster and stronger immune response to repeated exposure to an antigen, and this mechanism can confer lifelong immunity from certain pathogens, e.g. measles, chickenpox.

The activated helper T-cell also stimulates the cell-mediated immune response by activating cytotoxic T-cells. They are the only cell-killing T-cells, and they locate, bind to and then lyse infected cells. This prevents further reproduction of the pathogen and exposes the pathogen to the B-cell antibody response, hence increasing its success. Like B-cells, T-cells also produce memory T-cells to provide a faster immune reaction upon further contact with the specific antigen. Both B-cells and cytotoxic T-cells can be stimulated by free antigens in the blood or lymph fluid without the action of a helper T-cell.

The T-lymphocytes that make up the cell-mediated response move from their source in the bone marrow to the thymus gland in the upper chest to develop fully. Here they mature and differentiate into two classes; the regulator T-cells and the effector T-cells. Regulator T-cells are the helper T-cells and suppressor T-cells that control the activities of both T- and B-lymphocytes. The effector T-cells are the killer T-cells and delayed hypersensitivity T-cells. The killer T-cell is the only cell that kills the pathogen and infected cells. These B-cells remain and mature in the bone marrow and have the two classes; antibody-producing cells and memory cells. Speculation continues as to whether there is a set of regulatory B-cells that has not yet been found.

Without a healthy and effective immune system, the body would be considerably weakened and far more affected by everyday viruses or bacterial infections. It has long been known that vitamins and some trace elements are essential to the production of some immune cells, antibodies or chemical signals in the body, and continued medical research confirms this. Our daily requirement of vitamins may be small, but they have a considerable impact on the normal functioning of our immune system and energy metabolism.

Allergy and auto-immune diseases

Problems can arise with the immune system where it turns against itself. This leads to a series of auto-immune diseases, such as rheumatoid arthritis, Grave's disease or systemic lupus erythematosus (SLE). These problems can be especially difficult to treat or control.

Allergies occur because the body's defences are hypersensitive to some allergens in our environment. The inflammatory response releases histamines and other inflammatory agents into the bloodstream, and the person may start sneezing with a runny nose and even have breathing difficulties. Both the cell and antibody-mediated immune response overreact to antigens, producing an allergic reaction. Most allergens are things like pollen, dust (or more specifically the house dust mite), cats, dogs or horses. Food allergy also occurs and has a range of severity. The most severe form of allergic reaction is anaphylactic shock, when a person can have breathing difficulties, swelling of the throat, a drop in blood pressure and loss of consciousness. Here, death can occur within minutes unless adrenaline is administered to counteract the allergic response. This type of allergic reaction is fortunately fairly rare but can be caused by a bee or wasp sting or by eating nuts, especially peanuts, or shellfish.

At the other end of the scale, some people can be sensitive to some foods, and this may cause problems such as migraines, respiratory difficulties, tension, depression, joints and muscle aches, and headaches. Other conditions, such as hay fever symptoms, irritability, cramps, stomach upsets and indigestion, may also result from food intolerance. The most common type of food sensitivity is to dairy products or wheat. It may be difficult to pinpoint any specific food that triggers a reaction, but it may be worthwhile eliminating a suspect food from your diet for a time and seeing if the symptoms alleviate.

Some nutritional doctors believe that allergies can be treated and eased by supplementation with certain vitamins, minerals and essential fatty acids. Adults with an adverse reaction to pollen and dogs have had their symptoms removed by taking selenium and calcium tablets each day. Children allergic to horses and milk and suffering from asthma have been 'cured' of these problems by treatment with zinc, selenium and gamma-linolenic acid. Asthma patients treated in this manner have noticed a reduction in respiratory difficulties and in mucous formation in the lungs. In some cases, people have no longer required their normal medical treatment of steroid pills and inhalers. It must be noted that each case of allergy or asthma is treated individually, and benefits derived from nutritional supplements can vary. In asthma, inflammation of the bronchi plays a large part in the condition, and free radicals are known to be involved in inflammatory responses. Asthma and allergies are activated by prostaglandins and the immune system. People with allergies have higher levels of the antibody immunoglobulin E (IgE) in their bodies, which is under the control of the B-cells. The B-cells are also controlled by the T-cells, and it is the T-cells that weaken faster as we grow older. Thus, reduced activity of the T-cells, particularly a group called the suppressor T-cells, which normally tells an immune response to stop, is linked to autoimmune diseases and allergies, asthma and arthritis. So supplements to boost the functioning of the T-cells would be beneficial. Zinc can stimulate the hormone thymulin and interleukin-2, which both activate T-cells. Essential fatty acids such as gamma-linolenic acid, eicosapentanoic acid (EPA) and docosahexanoic acid (DHA) help regulate the protaglandin and leukotriene metabolisms and temper the inflammatory response. Antioxidants can be taken to fight the free radicals produced in the inflammatory response.

The role of vitamins, minerals and essential fatty acids in the immune system

Supplements of iron, selenium, zinc, copper, magnesium, vitamins A, C, D, E and B_6 along with gamma-linolenic acid, EPA and DHA can help to strengthen the immune system and prevent recurrent viral infections. The dosage needed is much greater than that found in our normal diets, but the benefits of fewer infections are well worth it. Children from six months to four years old were also given a range of supplements, and they had a reduced incidence of common infectious diseases such as ear infections, colds and sinusitis.

Vitamins and minerals are required for the formation and functioning of many immune cells. Deficiencies of vitamin A, B_1 (thiamin), B_3 (niacin) or C result in specific disease conditions, which can be resolved by sufficient intake of that vitamin. Viral and bacterial infections reduce the levels of vitamin A, B_6 and C in the body, and higher levels of vitamin B_2 (riboflavin) are eliminated during a fever. All the B vitamins and vitamin C are essential to the normal functioning of white blood cells in an inflammatory response. The defence mechanisms of the macrophages and the T- and B-lymphocytes require vitamins A, B_1, B_2, B_9 (folic acid), B_{12} and E to function well. Many vitamins, including A, B_6, B_9 and B_{12}, take part in making proteins and DNA, so lack of any of them can result in reduced resistance to disease. Vitamin B_6 (pyridoxine) encourages production of nucleic acids in cells that are crucial for growth and the production of antibodies. The thymus gland, where the T-lymphocytes are matured, also depends on vitamin B_6. Pyroxidine deficiency leads to fewer T- and B-lymphocytes in the blood and fewer antibodies produced. Lack of B_6 means neutrophil white blood cells are less able to ingest and destroy bacteria. Infants born to mothers with inadequate pyroxidine levels have a smaller spleen and thymus than normal children, so newborn children with deficiencies in vitamins may have a weakened cellular immunity. Up to a third of elderly people may lack enough vitamin B_6, and this can reduce their resistance to ageing and illness, and may even impair their mental functions. Lowered levels of antibody production may occur because of inadequate supplies of vitamin A, B_6, B_5 (pantothenic acid), B_9 and biotin.

Vitamins A, C and E help to protect the mucous membranes and the skin. Too little vitamin A can mean a smaller thymus and spleen, hence fewer white blood cells being produced. Children born with insufficient vitamin A are far more at risk from infectious diseases, and supplements given to children in Indonesia and Africa resulted in lowered child mortality. Care should be taken, as too much vitamin A is toxic and has the effect of weakening the immune system. Vitamin C's role is to make sure the skin is strong and to maintain the correct working of the neutrophils. It may be worthwhile increasing our intake of vitamin C during colds or influenza, for example, as the level of the vitamin in the macrophages falls, so impairing their ability to fight the pathogen. Lack of vitamin E weakens antibody formation, the activity of the lymphocytes, and causes changes in the delayed hypersensitivity reaction.

Certain minerals also have their part to play in the immune system. The metabolism of zinc changes when our bodies are fighting infection. The zinc is used to produce a protein that helps to protect our cells, but if the infection continues for a period of time we may become deficient in the mineral. A contributory factor is that the loss of zinc via the urine and excreta increases during an infection, and the uptake via the diet may be less because of lack of appetite. Since zinc is involved with the functioning of nearly 200 enzymes, lack of zinc can lead to all sorts of problems, including less energy being produced in the cells and no formation of nucleic acids. Zinc helps cells divide, so is vital to the proliferation and maturation of lymphocytes. Zinc is particularly important for the helper T-cells and the killer cells of the inflammatory response. Insufficient zinc affects the thymus in a similar manner to lack of vitamin A, with reduced hormone production but increased antibody formation.

Iron is necessary for the functioning of the lymph tissues and also for the correct activity of the neutrophils. Lack of iron can disrupt the immune system, damaging the cellular immunity, and occasionally the antibody levels may drop as well. Disruption to the immune system from lack of iron can occur when our intake is reduced by only 10 per cent. This may be because of an accompanying deficiency in vitamin B_9, folic acid. Iron forms part of enzyme proteins like transferrin and lactoferrin. These proteins scavenge all the available iron, so none is left for bacteria and they cannot grow. People suffering from long-term infections or inflammation are often anaemic and lacking iron. When given supplements, the anaemia is still present as the iron is taken into the blood serum and the tissues, not the red blood cells. When this occurs, the enzyme proteins are saturated with iron, and any pathogens can grow without restriction on the available iron. Thus, it actually increases the risk of developing new infections. In the case of some rheumatoid arthritis patients, they may have too much iron but their levels of haemoglobin in the blood are low. Here, the iron is held in the blood serum and tissues, and the number of red blood cells is dangerously low. This shows that iron supplementation may not always help fight disease.

During infections, the levels of copper (in the form of the protein ceruloplasmin) in the blood increase. This is believed to play a part in the body's defence mechanism but is not yet fully understood. Magnesium and calcium are both needed so that the metabolism of cell membranes can function normally. Lack of magnesium weakens formation of antibodies and leads to reduced size of the thymus gland. During infection, the levels of magnesium in the blood fall, and the body loses a lot of the calcium and magnesium that are released from the cells. Magnesium supplements would seem to be critical where a large amount of the mineral is lost because of serious burns or complications after an operation. The mineral helps the formation of complement proteins and acts to prevent allergies and common infections.

Lack of selenium reduces the cellular immune system, particularly if the person is deficient in vitamin E. Selenium allows the neutrophils to destroy antigens and boosts the activity of the T-lymphocytes. Inadequate selenium levels lead to increased lipid peroxidation in cell membranes, and deficiency of selenium and vitamin E at the same time increases the risk of developing cancer.

Vitamins and cancer

Cancer is a disease of disordered cell growth. Certain cells start uncontrolled growth to form a tumour that may invade surrounding tissues and spread by a process called metastasis to form secondary tumours in other parts of the body. Cancer develops in phases, starting with initiation, then promotion and progression to form a malignant tumour. Initiation occurs when DNA molecules inside a cell are attacked by a carcinogen. This substance can cause irreversible damage to DNA in a very short time. Some cancers develop without any damage being done to the DNA. The change in DNA that results is called a mutation. Carcinogens may be natural or synthetic in origin, and we are exposed to them in the air, sunlight, air pollution, our diet and our lifestyle. This damage to our DNA happens all the time, and in most of us our internal repair system prevents any problem developing and replaces the damaged DNA. If this does not occur, the disease can progress. This disease-causing initiation can occur often as a result of many tiny mutations that may occur day after day.

The next stage is the promotion phase. Here the cell with the mutation undergoes a number of chain reactions, which produce a cancer cell. The body loses control of the cell, which starts to divide uncontrollably. The tumour formed is a mass of genetically identical cells. Substances that promote cell division and proliferation can act as promoters. These include excessive oestrogen, arsenic, epoxides, excessive exposure to sunlight and lack of vitamin A. This promotion stage is called 'precancerous' by doctors. Progression or clonal evolution follows the promotion stage. Here the cell population in the tumour produces clones of cells, which are slightly different genetically from the original tumour and from each other. These cells have a high division rate; they move into other tissues and send out metastases (daughter tumours) to other areas of the body. When examined under a microscope, the cells look different and disorganized. Doctors call this dysplasia and say they are 'premalignant' as they have not infiltrated other tissues. When this occurs, they are considered malignant and cancerous. The promotion and progression phases are difficult, if not impossible, to separate as the process is a continuum that results in a fully developed cancer.

Cancer exists in many different forms, which are classified according to the cells that gave rise to them. The most common types are carcinomas of the skin, glands and the membranes lining the respiratory, urinary and gastrointestinal systems. Sarcomas develop from connective tissues, cartilage, muscles and membranes covering muscles and fat, and are less common. Lymphoma is cancer of the lymph nodes while leukaemia is a disease of the white blood cells. The treatment of each type is different as are the causes and specific progression of the disease. In the UK, the commonest cancers are of the lungs, the breasts and the skin. Around 90 per cent of all lung cancers are caused by smoking, and there is increasing evidence that passive smoking can contribute to developing the disease. Lung cancer is also difficult to cure, and only 10 per cent of patients survive for longer than 10 years. Skin cancer is easier to treat and has a higher success rate if the disease is caught early enough. There are 25,000 new cases a year, and this number is increasing as more people take sunshine holidays and are exposed to more ultraviolet light. There is the possibility that the reduced levels of ozone in the upper atmosphere is letting more ultraviolet light through to the ground, and this may result in more cancers developing.

Breast cancer is the most common cancer in Britain, killing 15,000 women a year. Routine examination is recommended to check for lumps, and a breast screening programme for women aged between 50 and 64 is currently under way. Breast cancer may be prevented by taking anti-oestrogen drugs such as tamoxifen, by breast-feeding, by a low fat diet, and some doctors believe that nipple stimulation encourages production of a hormone called oxytocin, which is normally produced during breast-feeding and may reduce the risks of developing breast cancer. Five to ten per cent of breast cancers are thought to be linked to genetics. Two genes that are linked to breast cancer development have been found, BRCA 1 and BRCA 2, and work is continuing to find the range of possible mutations and to develop a screening programme for these genes.

Although we are exposed to carcinogens in our diet, many dietary components can also help to protect us against cancer. For example, fibre absorbs carcinogens and fat in our diet, and takes them out of our body. A diet that is high in fibre also reduces the length of time for which the digested food is present in the large intestine, so reducing the amount of time that the colon and rectum are exposed to harmful substances. This is proven to reduce the incidence of colon and rectal cancers. Evidence shows that up to 40 per cent of all cancers may be caused by nutritional factors. This is partly because of the carcinogens in food but also because of insufficient intake of protective vitamins and minerals. Recent studies have proposed that deficiencies of beta-carotene, vitamins A, C and E and selenium could increase the risks of developing cancer. Many large-scale clinical studies are under way in both hemispheres to determine the effects of these and other micronutrients that may prevent cancer. Several nutritional doctors recommend supplements of 100µg of selenium (in the form of L-seleno-methionine) 30mg ubiquinone, 200–300mg of vitamin C, 200mg of vitamin E and 16,000–20,000 IU of beta-carotene per day. This may seem excessive but would have considerable benefits against not only cancer but also against heart disease and infectious diseases.

Many of these vitamins and minerals are also used in conjunction with chemotherapy and radiotherapy. Both these means of treating cancer can cause damage to our cells. Chemotherapy with cytotoxic drugs can kill cells other than the cancer cells and also triggers production of more free radicals in the body. Radiotherapy can kill the cancer cells but also may damage the genetic material in normal, healthy cells. These two treatments lower the levels of beta-carotene and vitamin E in the blood, so supplementation is required. There is some evidence to back the idea that beta-carotene, canthaxanthine (a provitamin of vitamin A), selenium, gamma-linolenic acid and fish oils may inhibit the proliferation of cancer cells and may also prevent or limit the development of metastases. Supplementation boosts the general condition of a person with cancer and can help the patient deal with the experience of chemotherapy or radiotherapy. Some doctors believe that supplements of the antioxidants, vitamin A, C, E, B_1, B_2, B_3, B_6 and manganese and magnesium, can help a patient deal with difficult treatments. Fish oils containing EPA and DHA, gamma-linolenic acid, selenium and some amino acids may be good in helping to fight cancer.

Healthy people can tolerate repeated initiations by carcinogens as the immune system and the antioxidant defence system can disable the harmful substances and repair the damaged cellular DNA.

Vitamins and heart disease

Heart diseases are the single largest killer in the UK and throughout the industrialized world. There are various forms of heart disease, the main examples being coronary thrombosis, cardiac arrhythmia, hypertension and chronic diseases of the heart valves. It may also be associated with diseases of the coronary arteries, the commonest of which is coronary arteriosclerosis. This is a progressive disease that may start developing before puberty. The arteries become narrowed by deposits of fat and oxidized fats that build up on the artery walls. These plaques harden and narrow the blood vessel, reducing the blood flow through it. The oxidized fats stop an enzyme called prostacyclin synthetase from working. The enzyme produces prostacyclin (PG12), which is normally found in the walls of the artery, and when levels of PG12 fall blood starts to clot in that area. Red blood cells in the clot rupture and release iron and copper, which stimulate oxidation and eventually lead to the formation of a blood clot. This clot can detach itself and move through the circulatory system, and it may become lodged in a blood capillary in the brain, heart or lungs. In arteriosclerosis, restricted blood flow through coronary arteries can lead to oxygen deficiency in the heart, which is known as angina pectoris. Symptoms of angina include breathlessness, dizziness and sweating with a dull pain or tightness in the chest. When the blood flow returns to normal, reperfusion of blood in the tissues occurs, and this can produce toxic-free radicals in the cells. These radicals can increase the levels of oxidized fats in the plaque. Many antioxidants in our diets can protect against these effects of free radicals and reduce the damage done to heart cells.

Antioxidants can also prevent heart failure, if given within three hours of a heart attack. So, if we improve our diet by reducing our intake of all fats, particularly saturated fats, and increase the levels of antioxidants in our bodies, then we can prevent or lessen the formation of plaques in our arteries and hence prevent blood clots and further damage. Vitamins A, C, E, B_6, along with beta-carotene, ubiquinone, selenium and zinc, all work to limit the action of oxygen radicals in the tissues of the heart and arteries. Ubiquinone (also called co-enzyme Q10) is very important in protecting the cardiac cells and is commonly prescribed to heart patients in Japan.

Many large studies have been carried out to monitor antioxidant levels in blood serum and to work out if there is a link between the antioxidant level in blood and the risk of coronary heart disease. It seems that the lower the level of antioxidant in blood, the higher the risk of death from myocardial infarction. Myocardial infarction is another term for ischaemic heart disease, or coronary heart disease. This disease results from blockage or narrowing of one of the coronary arteries, which reduces the blood supply to the heart, leading to oxygen deficiency and death of areas of heart tissue (myocardium). The heart can tolerate lack of oxygen and reperfusion of blood much better if it contains enough antioxidants. Cardiac arrhythmia may be caused by low levels of both potassium and magnesium in the blood. Tests of blood serum for these minerals do not reflect their true values, as most of the body's potassium and magnesium is found inside the cells. In some cases supplements of magnesium can help to reduce the severity of cardiac arrhythmia. Arrhythmia may also be eased by supplements of selenium, vitamins E and B_6.

Fish oils containing eicosapentaenoic acid (EPA) and docosahexanoic acid (DHA) are believed to help in cases of heart disease.

These oils are rich in omega-3 fatty acids, which decrease the tendency of blood platelets to clot in the blood vessels. They seem to reduce the levels of cholesterol in the blood and also lower the levels of fat or triglycerides in the blood. Fish oils are found in fatty fish such as herring, mackerel, tuna and salmon. They generally help prevent arteriosclerosis developing and reduce the chances of blood clots forming, which may block blood vessels. People with a diet rich in fatty fish (and so fish oils) have a reduced incidence of heart disease with far less mortality.

Vitamins

vitamin A

This is a fat-soluble vitamin that occurs naturally in animal products. It is actually a group of compounds including retinol, retinal, carotene and carotenoids. Retinol is the main active form of vitamin A, and it is proposed to have a hormonal function. The chemical structure of retinol was determined by Paul Karrer in 1931, and both natural and synthetic forms of vitamin A have been available for many years. The carotenes are precursors to vitamin A, and when ingested they are transformed into vitamin A in the liver. They are safer as they are nontoxic to humans and there is no risk of poisoning.

The active form of vitamin A is the aldehyde retinal, which is vital for the proper formation of rhodopsin, the light-sensitive pigment in vertebrate rod cells in the eye. The pigment is made up of retinal attached to the protein opsin. When light enters the eye and hits a rod cell, it stimulates a set of reactions in which rhodopsin separates back into its two components, and this triggers nervous activity in the rod cell and sends an image to the brain. The rhodopsin pigment reforms in darkness. This is why vitamin A is critical for good eyesight and why it prevents night blindness. In cases of vitamin A deficiency, various deleterious effects can occur. The epithelial tissues can atrophy, leading to conditions called keratomalacia and xerophthalmia. Keratomalacia is a condition in which the cornea in the eye is dry and ulcerated. This shows as night blindness, abnormal sensitivity to light, painful conjunctiva and red and swollen eyelids. It can eventually lead to blindness. Xerophthalmia is a similar condition in which the cornea and conjunctiva are dry and lustreless. Deficiency of vitamin A also leads to night blindness, defective development of the teeth, stunted growth, various skin eruptions, problems of the mucous membranes and reduced defence against infections. A lack of vitamin A in children in developing countries can cause ulceration of the eye, blindness and death.

Vitamin A is found in many foods, including butter, egg yolk, animal fats, liver, green vegetables, kidney, yellow/red fruits and yellow/orange vegetables. In the average diet, three-quarters of our vitamin A comes from retinol itself, while the rest comes from beta-carotene. Excess vitamin A is stored in the liver, and the vitamin has a half-life of between 200 and 300 days in the liver, so the vitamin A balance is only disturbed if intake is too low over a period of months. An estimated one million IU of stored vitamin A is found in each person, 90 per cent of that in the liver, 1.5 per cent in the blood and the rest contained in other tissues. The capacity for vitamin storage is reduced in cases of liver disease.

There is a possibility that vitamin A can be stored in such large quantities that it becomes toxic. Cases are recorded where vitamin poisoning has occurred with vitamins A and D, and this normally occurs with very high doses over long periods of time. Acute vitamin A poisoning was first seen more than 100 years ago in polar explorers, who ate polar bear liver and seal meat, which is very rich in vitamin A (> 10,000 IU per gram). They suffered from dizziness, nausea, headaches and vomiting, which are classic signs of acute vitamin A poisoning. Early symptoms of excess vitamin A are dry skin and itching. Doses of approximately 25,000 IU per day should be acceptable even over a long time period. There is a risk of vitamin A overdosing in pregnancy with a risk of foetal damage, but that has been with doses in excess of 20,000 IU per day. Several doctors state that it is perfectly safe, even during pregnancy, to take daily supplements of up to 8000 IU of vitamin A.

Recent research has indicated several new areas where vitamin A or beta-carotene are important in the body. Vitamin A and the carotenoid group have become an effective treatment for a number of skin diseases, including photosensitivity, where exposure to sunlight or ultraviolet light can cause oedema, acute burns, urticaria and skin lesions. Beta-carotene is an antioxidant that can stop excess oxidation of fats or lipids in cells. This appears to work via the cell's genetic material, either RNA or DNA, although the actual mechanism is not known. Beta-carotene also has a special affinity to an oxygen-free radical called singlet oxygen. This is a compound with an extra electron or proton that is unstable and readily reacts with other molecules in the body. Beta-carotene appears to react with the radical and removes it from the system. Beta-carotene can protect the skin from excessive sunlight, and this may result in a yellowing of the skin, which is not a result of overdosing on beta-carotene.

Prophylactic treatment with vitamin A and beta-carotene

Antioxidant vitamins and minerals found naturally in our diet can protect us against the harmful effects of free radicals, lipid peroxidation and even help prevent cancer. This may seem like an extreme statement, but it is now believed that most chronic and common diseases are caused by deleterious mutations in our DNA, most of which are caused by free radicals. So, if we take enough antioxidants into our bodies, we can support our immune system and perhaps prevent the occurrence of many diseases.

Low levels of vitamin A and beta-carotene in the blood are thought to be a risk factor in cancer, and so higher doses of these two chemicals are thought to have a prophylactic effect on cancers. This beneficial effect is increased when vitamin A is combined with vitamin E and the mineral selenium, which are also antioxidants. Vitamin A has been found to reinforce the immune system and increase survival rates of children in the Third World. Many epidemiological studies have found that a low blood serum level of beta-carotene would indicate a future risk of cancer. Beta-carotene levels in the blood appear to be reduced by smoking, which is also a risk in terms of lung cancer. A major study is currently under way of 52,000 people in Finland and the United States on the effects of diet supplementation with beta-carotene on disease levels.

Disease treatment

In underdeveloped countries around 50 million children have a deficiency of vitamin A. The World Health Organization and UNICEF are running large-scale projects in Africa and southeast Asia to try to overcome this. Mothers are given 200,000 IU and children get around 100,000 IU weekly, and so far the level of xerophthalmia and blindness has fallen by more than 80 per cent, and child mortality has fallen by 35 per cent. These periodic huge doses of vitamin A are not ideal, but it is effective in these difficult areas. Vitamin A helps in the renewal of skin cells and in replacement of the collagen (proteins in the connective tissues), so it has been given to help treat certain skin diseases. Acne can be helped with a daily intake of 100,000–200,000 IU over a period of weeks or months. The dosage is normally reduced after a few weeks. A vitamin A derivative called tretinon is used as a lotion, gel or cream and is often prescribed by doctors to treat acne with lesions, pustules and blackheads. Its use must be carefully monitored as the lotion can cause irritation of the eyes, nose and mouth, and there can be an adverse reaction to excess ultraviolet or sunlight exposure. It is a common and highly effective treatment in most cases.

Other skin diseases that can benefit from vitamin A treatment include psoriasis, where patients were given very high doses of up to 300,000 IU per day. This involved a risk of toxicity so a new derivative of vitamin A, called isotretinoid, has been used for treating psoriasis. These isotretinoid chemicals are actually thirty times more concentrated than vitamin A and are of particular risk if pregnant. The preparations are marketed as Retin-A lotion and as Roaccutane capsules, but they are available only on prescription. This new vitamin A product has also been used in some forms of cancer, e.g. T-cell leukaemia.

Vitamin A and beta-carotene are also given to cancer patients undergoing cytotoxic chemotherapy or radiotherapy. The treatment produces free radicals in the body, which are supposed to attack cancer cells, but they also damage normal tissue and reduce the level of natural antioxidant chemicals in the blood. Work carried out in Italy has shown that supplementation of beta-carotene with a vitamin A derivative called canthaxanthine has anti-cancer properties that may stop the formation of daughter tumours. Clinical studies are currently proceeding to examine these results more closely.

The recommended dietary allowances for vitamin A are 5000 IU in Europe and the USA, which equals about 1mg. The values of RDA are based on American figures, which were first calculated in 1943 and are updated every five years. They apply only to the healthy population and exclude babies, pregnant and nursing mothers, people with chronic or infectious diseases, people on permanent medication, people with metabolic disorders, smokers and people aged over 50. The RDAs are calculated with an inbuilt safety margin and are only the vitamin levels required to prevent well-known deficiency symptoms. Today, there is much more awareness of the preventative nature of vitamins and minerals, and doses well above RDA levels are common in preventing disease and boosting the immune system.

Beta-carotene itself can be considered an essential vitamin. It is a powerful antioxidant and a cancer prophylactic, with recommended blood serum levels set at 400 nano moles per litre. It can be given for hypersensitivity to light and photo-allergy, which can occur in the chronic disease known as systemic lupus erythematosus (SLE). Beta-carotene can also help absorb the free radicals produced by reperfusion in humans. Reperfusion is another name for the oxidation damage that occurs in cells that have been deprived of oxygen because of a reduced blood supply. When the blood flow returns to normal and the tissues are supplied with oxygen, some damage occurs because of the large amounts of oxygen radicals that are produced. These radicals can be neutralized by antioxidants, so reducing the level of damage caused to cells and also the impact on the cells. This type of oxidation damage is a risk in coronary heart disease, thrombosis, arteriosclerosis, brain circulatory disorders and in all types of surgery. It is a particular problem with hand or heart surgery where the circulation is stopped for a time and in transplant operations. There is a link between reperfusion injury and arrhythmia where reperfusion raises the number of oxygen radicals formed and they attack the fatty acids in the cell membranes to form toxic aldehydes and lipoxins, which can stimulate possibly fatal arrhythmia. Antioxidants including beta-carotene, selenium, etc, can inhibit the action of the oxygen radicals and stop any damage occurring in the heart cells.

vitamin B_1

thiamin, thiamine, aneurine

Vitamin B_1 is part of the vitamin B complex, and is water-soluble and hence easily lost during food preparation. Thiamin cannot be stored in the body in large quantities as there are only small reserve areas in the liver, heart and brain, and any excess is removed in the urine. The chemical structure of thiamin was discovered in 1936 by Robert Williams, and its main action in the body is in the formation of the enzyme thiamin pyrophosphate. This enzyme is required for the decarboxylation of certain acids in the Krebs cycle and is involved in the conversion of alanine to acetyl co-enzyme A, which is essential to the process. Thiamin also promotes normal metabolism, appetite, digestion and growth in the body, and it is also essential for the health of the cardiovascular and nervous systems. Thiamin also improves the functioning of T-cells and is required for normal development and functioning of the brain.

Deficiency of this vitamin can have a range of effects. It is thought that about half the population in industrialized countries suffers from minor long-term vitamin B deficiency. The RDA for thiamin is 1.5mg, but various factors increase the level required, e.g. pregnant women and elderly people need more thiamin per day. Factors such as stress, operations, alcohol, medicine, tobacco and carbohydrate consumption all affect the level of vitamin B_1 needed. Some of the thiamin taken into the body is not used for its original purpose, as it is consumed by alcohol, tobacco, stimulants such as coffee, and hormonal contraceptive pills. Minor deficiency may cause anxiety, irritability and depression, but the symptoms change as the deficiency becomes more severe. Ultimately, lack of thiamine leads to a disease called beriberi in which there is nerve inflammation with muscular weakness and heart failure. Loss of weight and appetite, disordered nerve function causing paralysis and wasting of limbs can also become part of the disease, which is common in Japan and other eastern areas. The disease is easily cleared up by a supplement of thiamin. Absorption of thiamin in the body occurs through the small intestine, and uptake of the vitamin is disrupted by disturbances in nutrient absorption, anorexia nervosa, chronic poor general health with diarrhoea and vomiting, and the use of diuretic medicines. Also, alcoholics often have thiamin deficiency, which can lead to weakening of the heart muscle and possibly heart failure.

Thiamin has no particular toxic effects, even in large doses of greater than 300 times the RDA. If given as an injection, vitamin B_1 can cause toxic symptoms like shaking, nervousness, swelling, disturbance of heart rhythm and allergic reactions. This may proceed further to disturb the functioning of the heart and nerves. These problems are resolved purely by cutting down the dose or stopping thiamin supplementation totally.

Thiamin is an antioxidant in humans, along with its fellow B vitamins—pantothenic acid B_5, B_3 niacin and B_2 riboflavin—and it is said to protect the cells from the chemical acetaldehyde, which is formed in cells by the action of free radicals. Acetaldehyde can cause mutations in DNA and cause cancer. Thiamin has been used as a medicine in skin diseases, disturbances in heart function, cancer, arteriosclerosis and arthritis to remove the free radicals produced by those diseases. Thiamin can also benefit a smoker's cough, seasickness, toothache and other minor pains. The B vitamins are synergistic in effect, i.e. they reinforce each other's effects on the body, and hence thiamin is best taken as part of a vitamin B complex supplement.

The best sources of thiamin are yeast, grain husks, whole-wheat products, peas, beans, potatoes, nuts, liver, eggs and pork. Deficiency can result from poorly milled or polished rice, which has lost most of its vitamin B_1 content.

vitamin B_2

riboflavin, lactoflavin, vitamin G

Vitamin B_2 or riboflavin is a water-soluble vitamin that can be partially decomposed by heat and sunlight. It was first detected in 1879 by Blyth, and its structure was isolated in 1935 by Paul Karrer and Richard Kuhn, among others. The vitamin has a crystalline structure and is yellow-orange in colour.

Riboflavin is found in various foodstuffs, including milk, liver, eggs, cheese, fish, yoghurt, green vegetables, pulses and yeast extract. Deficiencies of this vitamin can occur in pregnant mothers, nursing women, the elderly, slimmers, vegans and the chronically ill. Lack of riboflavin can be caused by diseases such as arthritis and tuberculosis, and by the action of drugs like antibiotics, tranquillizers, contraceptive pills and sulpha products. Vitamin B_2 in the body is absorbed by the small intestine, and the process is regulated by thyroid gland hormones. Thus some antidepressants and nerve medicines can affect the thyroid and disrupt absorption of the vitamin. Riboflavin is largely stored in our red blood cells, and reserves in the human body seem to be fairly stable, with any excess being eliminated in the urine or excreta. Vitamin B_2 deficiency can result in inflammation of the tongue and lips, scaly scalp and eczema, hair loss, dizziness, insomnia, hacks in the corner of the mouth and oversensitivity to light. Some studies indicate that riboflavin deficiency is the commonest vitamin deficiency in industrialized countries, with 20 per cent of people suffering from it. Riboflavin has an important role in energy release from carbohydrates, in that it forms part of two co-enzymes called flavine adenine dinucleotide (FAD) and flavine mononucleotide (FMN). These chemicals are involved in the metabolism of all nutrients as well as being two critical components of the oxidative phosphorylation reactions of the electron transport chain. This means that the food eaten is broken down efficiently and the maximum energy is obtained from it.

Riboflavin is also involved in the production of the brain neurotransmitters serotonin, noradrenaline and acetylcholine and in histamine, which is released from tissue cells after damage. It is also connected to the synthesis of the three essential fatty acids required by humans—linoleic acid, linolenic acid and arachidonic acid. Riboflavin inhibits the production of chemicals called leukotrienes and prostaglandins. Prostaglandins are a group of unsaturated fatty acids that are found in most mammalian tissues. They have a wide range of activity on the body, including regulation of cell function and fertility. They lower blood pressure and cause contraction of smooth muscle. They are released after tissue damage as part of the inflammatory response and can cause painful muscle cramps in some people.

There is very little risk of overdosing on riboflavin as the upper limit is 3g per kilogram of body weight per day and the RDA is 1.3mg–1.7mg per day. Extremely large doses can cause numbness and itching in some cases.

vitamin B_3

niacin, nicotinic acid, nicotinamide, nicotinate; chemical name: pyridine-3-carboxylic acid, C_5H_4NCOOH

Unlike vitamins B_1 and B_2, niacin can be produced in the body from the essential amino acid tryptophan. This only occurs in small amounts so most of the human requirements are met in our diet. Niacin is a white, crystalline vitamin that is water-soluble and hence vulnerable to destruction by heat, strong light and low temperatures.

Vitamin B_3 is contained in meat, poultry, liver, kidney, eggs, nuts, fish, cheese, peas, beans, milk, dried fruit, yeast extract and some cereals, e.g. rice. It is found as two different forms—nicotinic acid and its amide, nicotinamide, both of which are active in the body. Niacin has various beneficial actions, and it is critical to food metabolism and the breakdown of glucose in the Krebs cycle. Niacin is used biosynthetically to derive the co-enzyme nicotinamide adenine dinucleotide (NAD), which is essential to a large number of oxidation reduction reactions that occur in the breakdown of glucose and fatty acids to release energy. NAD also exists as NADP, with an additional phosphate group. Niacin also plays a part in maintenance of the nervous system, normal functioning of the gastrointestinal tract, maintenance of healthy skin, and synthesis of the sex hormones. It also aids efficient blood circulation by expanding the arteries and reducing resistance to blood flow. Niacin is known to remove low-density lipoprotein cholesterol from the blood. This LDL-cholesterol is the dangerous form of cholesterol that increases the risk of hardening of the coronary arteries. This suggests that niacin may be beneficial in preventing heart disease.

Other therapeutic uses of niacin are to treat dizziness and contracted blood vessels, as well as using niacin in conjunction with other B complex vitamins to reduce fluid loss from the body associated with burns. Vitamin B_3 has been used in the United States as a substitute for sleeping pills, and it has been utilized as a tranquillizing drug in schizophrenia, alcoholism and migraine, combined with vitamin C. Niacin also shares an antioxidant effect with other members of the B complex vitamins.

The RDA for niacin is 18mg per day, but more is needed by men, pregnant women and breast-feeding women. More niacin is required by the body if the vitamins B_1 (thiamin), B_2 (riboflavin) and B_6 (pyridoxine) are deficient as these vitamins help in the conversion of tryptophan to niacin. The formation of niacin would seem to be inhibited by contraceptive pills. Two-thirds of the niacin we use is produced from tryptophan in the diet. Deficiency in niacin produces a wide range of symptoms, including muscle weakness, fatigue, loss of appetite, skin eruptions, irritability, nausea, vomiting, recurring headaches, tension, depression and insomnia. Severe niacin deficiency results in a disease called pellagra, which still occurs in slum areas of developed countries, in developing countries and in alcoholics. The characteristics include scaly dermatitis, inflammation of the mucous membranes, diarrhoea and mental disturbances that can include depression, confusion, delirium, disorientation and dementia. Ultimately, without niacin supplementation, the sufferer will die.

vitamin B_5

pantothenic acid, pantothenate

Pantothenic acid is a water-soluble vitamin that is required by most higher organisms for efficient functioning of the body. The structure of pantothenic acid was isolated in 1940 by J. R. Williams, who named the vitamin pantothenate. Vitamin B_5 is quite heat-resistant and is not destroyed by frying, cooking or baking, but it is lost in food cooked in a pressure cooker (because of the high temperatures) and in deep-frozen meat. Pantothenic acid is found in almost all foods, including beans, eggs, liver, whole-grain cereals, oranges, peanuts, wheat germ and fish. It is produced in the human gut by intestinal bacteria, but this does not meet the total amount of pantothenic acid required by the body. Pantothenic acid from the diet is absorbed in the stomach and small intestine, but very little vitamin B_5 is stored in the body, and it generally passes through the body unaltered. It is eliminated in the urine and excreta.

Pantothenic acid is essential for the metabolism of sugars, fats and proteins, as it forms part of co-enzyme A. This co-enzyme plays a very important role in the transfer of acetyl groups from various compounds in the Krebs cycle. Vitamin B_5 is also important in the formation and growth of new cells that are required for healthy skin and hair, and in the production of essential fatty acids. It is needed for the normal functioning of the steroid hormone cortisone, and it allows the body to use the vitamin-like substances choline and para-aminobenzoic acid (PABA). Pantothenic acid's most important role is in the functioning of the B-lymphocytes, which are critical for the production of antibodies. Thus pantothenic acid plays a large role in cell defence against disease. As co-enzyme A, pantothenic acid is distributed throughout all body tissues, concentrating in the liver, heart and kidneys where large quantities of energy are required for proper functioning of the tissue. The blood levels of vitamin B_5 are usually between 100 and 400g per litre, and the RDA for vitamin B_5 is 10mg.

Vitamin B_5 deficiency is exceedingly rare in humans, and generally is found only in experimental conditions where volunteers are given a pantothenic acid-free diet. Under these conditions, symptoms that are seen include asthma, muscle cramps, insomnia, fatigue, stomach pain, numbness in the limbs, personality changes, discomfort, reduced antibody production, and increased susceptibility to allergy and infection. These problems are rectified by taking a supplement of pantothenic acid.

Pantothenic acid is also important in other species, e.g. birds and rats. In chickens, a lack of vitamin B_5 causes dermatitis and nerve degeneration in the spinal cord, and pantothenic acid is known as chick anti-dermatitis factor. In rats that are given pantothenic acid-free diets, the body hair loses pigmentation and turns grey. This effect has been reversed in some cases and pigmentation was returned to the hair. This occurrence did not provide firm evidence of a link between hair pigmentation and pantothenic acid in the diet in rats, and there is no evidence that a similar effect could occur in humans.

Salts of pantothenic acid have been used to treat various medical disorders. Sodium and potassium salts are used to help circulatory problems in the legs, including 'restless legs'. The calcium salt has been a good therapy for a condition called paralytic ileus in which a patient is unable to move for a long time after an operation. The salt is generally administered as an injection, with a very high dose of up to 1000mg being given. The vitamin aids the system as it improves the activity and peristalsis of the small intestine. Pantothenic acid ointments may be used to treat skin injuries and burns.

Most people will receive sufficient vitamin B_5 through their diet and supplements should not be required.

vitamin B_6

pyridoxine, pyridoxal, pyridoxamine, $C_8H_{11}NO_3$

Pyridoxine is a white, crystalline vitamin that forms part of the B complex group. It is water-soluble and was first isolated in its crystalline form in 1938. The precise structure of vitamin B_6 was deduced by Richard Kuhn in 1939. Pyridoxal and pyridoxamine are both related compounds with similar activity to the B_6 compound pyridoxine. In some species of bacteria the term pyridoxamine is preferred as the B_6 vitamin. Vitamin B_6 is required by most animals and bacteria species. The vitamin is found in many foods, including green vegetables, brewer's yeast, fish, pulses, milk, meat, liver, whole-grain cereals, nuts, raisins and prunes.

The vitamin has a very large range of actions in the body. Vitamin B_6 is essential for maintaining healthy skin and nerves, in the formation of red blood cells, in providing general resistance to disease, and to stop premature ageing. When taken into the body, pyridoxine is absorbed through the intestines and is rapidly metabolized and dispersed through the tissues. Monitoring of levels of vitamin B_6 can be done using whole blood, red blood cells or blood plasma, as they all reflect the patient's pyridoxine status. RDA values for vitamin B_6 are 2mg for women and 2.2mg for men. Greater B_6 requirements are seen in pregnant and breast-feeding women, people on a high protein diet, including athletes, people with chronic diseases, women on the contraceptive pill, and people with intestinal diseases, e.g. gluten allergy. In studies in Finland, up to 30 per cent of elderly residents in nursing homes were found to be deficient in vitamin B_6. The major functions of this vitamin include enzyme reactions, the formation of brain hormones, the formation of haemoglobin, and the maintenance of the homoeostatic balance of sodium and potassium ions in the body. Pyridoxine forms part of the pyridoxal diophosphate chemical, which is a prosthetic group associated with transamination reactions occurring in the mitochondria or cytosol of a cell. The chemical is important in allowing transaminase enzymes to function effectively, when they catalyse the conversion of alpha-amino acids into slightly different alpha-keto acids. This process is very important in the breakdown and synthesis of amino acids in the body. Vitamin B_6 is important in allowing the conversion of tryptophan in the diet into vitamin B_3 (niacin) and in the breakdown of glucose to a different form—glucose-1-phosphate—in the glycolysis process.

The vitamin is known to promote formation of hormones that are important in brain function, to encourage proper absorption of vitamin B_{12} (cyanocobalamin), to help the body utilize magnesium, and to be involved in the production of hydrochloric acid in the stomach. Vitamin B_6 improves the activity of both Band T-lymphocytes in our immune system, and this in turn helps to prevent diseases such as asthma, arthritis, cancer, coronary heart disease, various allergies and circulatory disorders. It regulates the ionic balance between sodium and potassium ions, allows proper uptake and use of the mineral selenium in the body, and partially controls the functioning and repair of the nervous and musculo-skeletal systems. Pyridoxine is essential for the formation of the haem group in haemoglobin, and it may also act to reduce the cholesterol level in the blood. The production of antibodies occurs because of vitamin B_6, and it also acts to stop aggregation of blood platelets in blood vessels, which commonly cause blood clots. The vitamin may provide protection against arteriosclerosis and heart attacks as it prevents the formation of plaque in artery walls. This occurrence has been seen in studies of monkeys and rabbits, and it is now confirmed in humans. Indeed, the action of vitamin B_6 resembles the action of essential fatty acids, in that deficiency symptoms are similar, and these symptoms can be cured using supplements of either substance. The precise mechanism for these beneficial effects of vitamin B_6 and EFAs are not known.

In some cases of acute heart attack, investigation showed that the patients had low levels of vitamin B_6 in their bodies. Some people have an hereditary condition that means they need an increased daily intake of vitamin B_6. This generally appears in the first few months after birth when the vitamin-deficient baby may suffer from epilepsy-like convulsions, but these frightening symptoms can be removed by pyridoxine supplementation. Deficiency in vitamin B_6 can result in loss of appetite, anaemia, emaciation, depression, fatigue, general apathy, nervousness, insomnia and poor memory. Symptoms can also include atrophy of the skin epidermis, hair follicles and sebaceous glands, oral cavity infections, hacks in the corners of the mouth, and a loss of the sense off touch in the limbs. These symptoms may indicate that other B vitamins are deficient from the diet, e.g. B_2 and B_{12}. Children and infants are more at risk from pyridoxine deficiency, when they can suffer from irritability, convulsions and anaemia.

For women, vitamin B_6 deficiency may be associated with discomfort and pain during menstruation and pregnancy. Lack of pyridoxine can be found in people with a high alcohol consumption, in women on the contraceptive pill, in elderly people and pregnant women. Vitamin B_6 can help to stabilize the blood/sugar balance during pregnancy and possibly to prevent the onset of diabetes during pregnancy.

Some medicines such as penicillamine (to prevent arthritis) and some tuberculosis medicines are antagonistic to vitamin B_6 and counteract its effects. This can lead to deficiency symptoms like drowsiness, convulsions and difficulty in walking. These problems can be resolved with supplements of 30–100mg per day in most cases, but symptoms related to the nervous system may only be stopped with a dosage of between 300 and 600mg. per day. As a therapeutic remedy, pyridoxine is given to patients with intestinal diseases, cancer, asthma and after major intestinal surgery at a dose of 50–150mg. Angina pectoris can be treated with between 100 and 300mg of B_6 per day, as can people recovering after a heart attack. This can be of particular benefit when combined with the mineral selenium, as the two nutrients act to reduce blood platelet accumulation, and the chances of blood clots are also reduced. Vitamin B_6 can be of great benefit to asthma sufferers, especially when given along with antioxidants and essential fatty acids. Very large doses of more than 1000mg can be dangerous and cause poisoning and damage to the peripheral nervous system, including disturbing the sense of touch. Vitamin B_6 is also given as a supplement to ease painful periods, premenstrual syndrome and in endometriosis.

vitamin B_9

folic acid, folate, vitamin B_9, folacin; pteroyl-L-glutamic acid, $C_{19}N_7O_6H_{14}$

Folic acid is a water-soluble vitamin, which has a yellow crystalline structure. In humans, a small amount is produced by intestinal bacteria, but this may not be sufficient. It was discovered by Dr Lucy Wills in 1931 while she was researching into a form of anaemia in India. She found that the addition of yeast to the patient's diet cured the anaemia, and folic acid was finally isolated in 1941. The name folic acid is from the Latin *folicum* for 'leaf', as the vitamin was isolated from spinach leaves. Indeed, spinach, asparagus, green vegetables, liver, yeast, kidneys, nuts and whole grains are among the best natural sources of folic acid. The role of vitamin B_9 in our bodies is as a precursor of tetrahydrafolic acid, which is a co-enzyme that transfers single carbon groups in enzyme reactions. This allows the formation of purines and pyrimidines, which are essential to the formation of nucleic acids such as DNA (deoxyribonucleic acid). New nucleic acids are made when new cells are being produced, and hence folic acid is required to produce red blood cells and in new cell synthesis in tissue repair. The co-enzyme also allows the formation of the amino acids serine and glycine. This enzymatic role of vitamin B_9 occurs in conjunction with vitamin B_{12} (cyanocobalamin), and they are both required in rapidly dividing cells for protein and nucleic acid formation. Vitamin C is also involved in the formation of the haem grouping in haemoglobin, like vitamin B_6 pyridoxine.

Vitamin B_9 is also said to increase the appetite and stimulates production of hydrochloric acid in the digestive system. Some sources state that folic acid may help protect women against cervical dysplasia, which are precancerous changes in the cells of the uterine cervix. Folic acid and its derivatives are very important to the formation of new cells and hence to the growth and development of the human embryo. The normal RDA for folic acid is 400µg, and both prior to and during pregnancy, women should have around 800µg folic acid per day to help prevent dietary deficiencies that may lead to neural tube defects in the embryo, e.g. spina bifida. Women who have previously given birth to a child with a neural tube defect, or if there is a family history of children with neural tube defects, then the women should be placed on supplements of 4mg per day. Mouth deformities such as a cleft palate or hair lip may also be caused by folic acid deficiency during pregnancy. Folic acid is passed on to a newborn baby via a mother's breast milk.

Folic acid deficiency can occur in many people, and it is said to be the commonest vitamin deficiency in the world. Up to 45 per cent of people may be low in vitamin B_9, and it is a particular problem in elderly people. The vitamin is rapidly destroyed by cooking, so maintaining an adequate intake can be a problem in hospital or institutional environments where food is kept warm for a period of time with a subsequent loss in vitamin levels. Folic acid in the diet is absorbed through the small intestine, and some cycling from the bile back to the intestine occurs. Thus any problems in production of bile upsets the folic acid balance in the body. Humans hold very small reserves of folic acid in the body, and the folic acid balance can be monitored via whole blood, red blood cells or blood serum tests. Deficiency in vitamin B_9 is seen in people with high alcohol consumption, in elderly people on inadequate diets, in pregnant women, in women on contraceptive pills, and in people who fast. Problems with the intestine can lead to malabsorption of food and vitamins with possible deficiency symptoms. Too little folic acid can lead to the development of megaloblastic anaemia, which covers several types of anaemia, including pernicious anaemia. This disease was previously fatal until it was discovered in 1926 that the disease was caused by the malabsorption of vitamin B_{12} (cyanocobalamin). These megaloblastic anaemias occur in 20 per cent of expectant mothers and can also be seen in children. Insufficient folic acid has been found in 24 per cent of surgical hospital patients in Britain, where the deficiency produced symptoms of depression, apathy, oral cavity infections, respiratory problems, dizziness and grey coloration to the skin. Vitamin B_9 and its absorption in the body is adversely affected by epilepsy medicines such as phenytoin or phenobarbital. Long-term loss of appetite or chronic diseases like gluten allergy can mean there is insufficient folic acid intake with possible deficiency problems such as forgetfulness, confusion, insomnia, shortness of breath, irritability and weakness.

Several medicines are antagonistic to folic acid, such as drugs that treat cancer or urinary system complaints. These can prevent the proper use of vitamin B_9 and create deficiency symptoms. As a remedy, folic acid supplements can be taken by patients with anaemia and rheumatoid arthritis. In people who have had surgical removal of their stomach, careful monitoring of levels of folic acid and cyanocobalamin is required to maintain their health.

vitamin B_{12}

cyanocobalamin, cyanocobalamine, $C_{63}H_{90}CoN_{14}O_{14}P$

Vitamin B_{12} is a water-soluble vitamin that contains cobalt, a cyanide group, and a nucleotide in its structure. It is dark red in colour with a crystalline structure, and was first isolated in 1948. The action of vitamin B_{12} is linked to vitamin B_9 (folic acid) and insufficient supplies of either causes deficiency symptoms. Cyanocobalamin forms part of the vitamin B complex, and it is found in animal food sources, e.g. liver, fish, eggs, meat, kidney, dairy products (particularly cheese), fortified cereals and brewer's yeast. Vitamin B_{12} is absorbed only from the gastrointestinal tract in the presence of the intrinsic factor, which is a glycoprotein produced by the intestinal epithelium. Without the intrinsic factor and calcium, the vitamin cannot be absorbed through the intestinal mucous membranes and enter the bloodstream. The resulting vitamin deficiency can cause pernicious anaemia, brain damage and degeneration of the nervous system. Until the 20th century, pernicious anaemia had no known cause, and it always produced fatal results. In 1926 G. R. Minot and W. P. Murphy found that the disease could be treated with liver, and this introduced the critical factor required for red blood cell production into the body. This extrinsic factor essential for the formation of red blood cells is vitamin B_{12}. Today, people with pernicious anaemia need to take vitamin B_{12}, normally in the form of injections, every three months for the rest of their lives. Deficiency of B_{12} affects nearly all the tissues of the body, particularly those with rapidly dividing cells, e.g. bone marrow and gamete production. Other actions of cyanocobalamin include influencing the activity of B- and T-lymphocytes, acting on neural function, and in the biosynthesis of the amino acid methionine and the vitamin-like substance choline. A chemical called 5–deoxyadenosyl cobalamin has co-enzyme activity and is required to synthesize nucleotides, to maintain the protein myelin surrounding the nerves, to allow correct erythrocyte maturation and to permit the correct functioning of folic acid (vitamin B_9) in the body. The co-enzyme form also works in protein formation, in preventing cell degeneration and in the metabolism of fats, carbohydrates and proteins to produce energy.

Deficiency of vitamin B_{12} does not only cause pernicious anaemia but it also produces tongue infections, disturbances of the nervous system such as loss of sensation and poor coordination. Continuing lack of cyanocobalamin produces fatigue, irritability, loss of appetite, diarrhoea, stomach complaints, problems with the circulation and heart with the skin colour becoming yellow. Menstrual disturbances, an unpleasant body odour, neuritis and numbness or tingling in the hands and feet may occur in a sufferer. Symptoms of pernicious anaemia can include additional mental problems such as loss of concentration, depression, paranoia and irritation. Many people with this disease show changes in the pattern of electrical impulses in the brain, which may be because of damaged myelin in the nerve endings. An interesting point is that 2 per cent of all psychiatric patients suffer from pernicious anaemia.

vitamin B_{15}

pangamate, pangamic acid

Whether this substance is a vitamin or provitamin is the subject of great debate. It was first isolated from apricot kernels in 1951, and it is also found in rice husks, horse liver, ox blood, brewer's yeast, maize and other plants. It was discovered by E. T. Krebs, who is said to have believed that pangamate has all-powerful properties. The chemical name for pangamate is glucono-dimethyl acetylate, and it is proposed to be a cure for alcoholism, hepatitis, cancer, diabetes and other diseases as well as being an antidote to toxins. Active research into the compound has been carried out in the former Soviet Union, but most government agencies, e.g. American Food and Drug Administration (FDA), do not believe there is enough evidence to show this substance is beneficial to health.

vitamin B_{17}

amygdalin, laetrile, $C_{20}H_{27}NO_{11}$

This substance is a naturally occurring glycoside that is found in most fruits of the *Rosaceae* family, particularly almonds and apricots. The reputation of this compound is better than that of pangamate, but it is unsure whether amygdalin is a vitamin or not. The substance has the chemical formula $C_{20}H_{27}NO_{11}$, which includes a C=N cyanide group, and it can be hydrolysed to produce benzaldehyde, glucose and hydrogen cyanide. Some sources suggest that amygdalin has a cancer-preventative effect. In some cases, amygdalin is taken by people to treat cancer only when they are on a diet that may help prevent cancer. The diet is mostly fruit and nuts with very high doses of minerals. The anti-cancer effects are said to be because of the production of hydrogen cyanide (HCN) in the tissues, which attacks and destroys cancer cells. Unfortunately, the hydrogen cyanide also kills healthy cells and is one of the most potent poisons known to man. Studies to try and determine the effects of amygdalin have had conflicting results, but many researchers now believe that amygdalin can cause cyanide poisoning or even cancer. Laetrile is the trade name given to amygdalin, and there may still be some limited use for amygdalin in alterative medicine.

vitamin C

ascorbic acid

Vitamin C is a white crystalline vitamin that was first isolated in 1932 by Charles Glen King. It was first synthesized artificially in 1933 by Tadeus Reichstein. It is water-soluble but is easily destroyed by cooking and contact with alkalis, and it can be easily oxidized. Ascorbic acid is also lost to some degree if food is deep-frozen or preserved. It is present in citrus fruit, berries, tomatoes, fresh green vegetables, potatoes, peppers, broccoli, cauliflower, some fruit juices and chillies. For healthy adults, an RDA of 60mg is recommended, with pregnant women requiring a higher intake. This intake would allow reserves of around 1500mg to build up in the body. An increased daily intake is needed for smokers, people on contraceptive pills or living in very hot or very cold environments. In Scandinavia, for example, deficiency diseases of vitamin C, such as scurvy, are still a problem in the long winter months as the body's reserves become depleted and there is little in the way of fresh fruit and vegetables to replace the body's stored supply. Various problems can arise from lack of vitamin C, depending upon the severity of the deficiency. The most severe disease is scurvy, which was common among sailors in the days of sailing ships, when fresh fruit and vegetables were not available on a long voyage and vitamin depletion occurred. Symptoms of scurvy start with swelling, inflammation and bleeding of the gums, often with loss of teeth, followed by haemorrhages under the skin, muscular weakness and serious joint damage because of haemorrhages. Over time, the disease causes anaemia, mouth ulceration and induration of the leg muscles. Milder deficiencies show up as tender joints, bleeding or soft gums, fatigue, weakness, reduced immunity to infections, irritability and muscle degeneration.

These deficiency problems illustrate that vitamin C is essential for the formation of collagen and connective tissues, and for production of the fibrous material found in the intercellular matrices in bone and teeth. Collagen is used for the formation of skin ligaments, tendons and cartilage. Ascorbic acid is also important for maintaining the strength of capillary walls and for aiding the absorption of iron, and it is needed to produce stress hormones. Vitamin C also improves resistance to infection and helps fight diseases such as high blood pressure, cancer and arteriosclerosis. Ascorbic acid is known to act as a co-factor in the oxidation of the amino acid tyrosine, and it may take part in oxidation-reduction reactions in energy metabolism.

Like many other vitamins and minerals, vitamin C has protective properties if taken in larger doses. Vitamin C is an antioxidant and, more importantly, it has a reinforcing influence in the period of activity and effects of other antioxidants, e.g. vitamins A and E. These three vitamins have a synergistic relationship, in that they increase each other's effects in the body. Ascorbic acid has a particularly important function in the brain as it protects against the effects of ischaemia or oxygen deficiency. This deficiency and the subsequent reperfusion of the area produce oxygen-free radicals that can destroy cells. In the body, the highest levels of vitamin C are to be found in nerve tissues and the brain, which are those most at risk from free radical damage.

This beneficial antioxidant action of vitamin C can be reversed if the vitamin itself is oxidized. When vitamin C is exposed to light, heat or air, a chemical called dehydroascorbate (DHA) is formed. This substance has a completely different effect from vitamin C—it is a pro-oxidant that encourages the production of oxygen-free radicals, leading to cell damage. Oxidation of vitamin C also occurs when it contacts iron or copper within the food. Mainly, the vitamin is protected by the cell membranes, but if they are removed by cooking then the vitamin C is attacked by the metals and is lost or transformed to dehydroascorbate.

Vitamin C, like vitamin A and selenium, is thought to be able to prevent the formation and development of cancer. When taken in large doses, vitamin C can prevent nitrites and nitrates in our foodstuffs from being converted into nitrosamines. Most of these nitrosamines are carcinogenic and can lead to the development of stomach cancer or cancer of the intestinal tract. This cancer-preventing action may extend to cancer of the throat or womb and malignant melanomas.

A further protective effect of vitamin C is that the vitamin improves the function of white blood cells called phagocytes. The role of the phagocytes in humans is to find, destroy and consume viruses, bacteria and cancer cells. Vitamin C also activates white blood cells called neutrophils and increases the level of antibodies found in the blood, in connection with elevated levels of the cellular protein interferon, which attacks viruses.

Ascorbic acid can help to prevent or lessen allergic reactions as it inhibits the action of histamine. Histamine is normally released when there is an allergic reaction in the respiratory passages, the skin or in the mucous membranes in the nose, and can lead to itching, rash formation, runny nose and breathing difficulties. Thus, vitamin C can lessen these symptoms and help in self-treatment of allergies. In some rare cases, vitamin C itself can trigger an allergic reaction.

Vitamin C acts along with vitamin B_1 (thiamin) and the amino acid cysteine to prevent the chemicals formalin, formaldehyde and acetaldehyde causing damage to the body. These harmful chemicals are produced by the breakdown of alcohol in the body or by tobacco smoke. Other chemicals that vitamin C acts against include nicotine, nitrogen compounds, vehicle exhaust fumes, and the toxic heavy metal cadmium. This explains why alcoholics or smokers have much lower levels of vitamin C in their blood, as it is consumed by these toxic substances. Supplements of vitamin C, selenium, zinc, beta-carotene, vitamins A and E and ubiquinone may help counterbalance some of the harmful effects of smoking.

Another vital protective role of vitamin C is in protecting heart muscle after a heart attack. Research has found that the white blood cells transport large quantities of vitamin C from other parts of the body to the heart. This could mean that other tissues become deficient in vitamin C, and blood levels could fall without adequate vitamin C supplementation. Vitamin C has the same role when the coronary arteries undergo hardening and narrow. Ascorbic acid also prevents and repairs cell damage in the blood vessels of the heart, and intravenous injections of vitamin C can reduce the chances of blood platelet aggregation, hence reducing the risk of blood clots.and arteriosclerosis.

Vitamin C may influence the balance between 'good' (HDL-) cholesterol and 'bad' (LDL-) cholesterol to increase levels of the HDL-cholesterol, and may be involved in preventing high blood pressure and arteriosclerosis, according to studies carried out in Finland. Large-scale research done by the World Health Organization showed that antioxidants, including vitamin C, inhibited the LDL-cholesterol from oxidizing into oxidized cholesterol, which forces itself into artery walls and is involved in the formation of arteriosclerosis. So vitamin C can prevent dangerous forms of cholesterol developing and reduces levels of the LDL-cholesterol.

Supplements of vitamin C normally cause few problems, but doses of several grams per day can lead to stomach problems in some people. This can normally be avoided if a soluble vitamin C tablet is taken or if the supplement is taken after meals. It is best to work your way up gradually to a large dose of vitamin C, as sudden high intakes can cause diarrhoea. On the other hand, stopping large doses of vitamin C suddenly is not advisable as it can lead to feelings of fatigue. The dose taken each day should be reduced gradually if a person wishes to stop taking large doses of vitamin C.

vitamin D

D_2 ergocalciferol/calciferol, D_3 cholecaliferol

This vitamin is actually a related group of hormone-like chemicals called steroid alcohols. Vitamin D_1 was the first to be discovered and turned out to be a crude mixture of steroid alcohols. Ergocalciferol is the name given to vitamin D_2, and it is produced from the provitamin ergosterol in plants. The conversion occurs because of the action of ultraviolet light on the chemical. Vitamin D_3 or cholecalciferol is derived from the provitamin dehydrocholesterol, which is widely distributed in the skin. When sunlight or ultraviolet light encounters the provitamin, it causes a change into the active form of it. In humans, vitamin D_3 may also be formed in milk when it is exposed to sunlight.

The group of vitamin D chemicals was first isolated as crystals in 1931. Both vitamins D_2 and D_3 are white, crystalline alcohols, and they differ only in the structure of their chemical side chains and in their melting points. These minor changes still mean that both forms have almost identical actions. Vitamin D is fat-soluble and is found in animal fats, butter, eggs, liver, fish (particularly kippers, mackerel, sardines and tuna), margarine, full-fat dairy products, malted milk drinks and evaporated milk. Milk is rich in vitamin D only if it is fortified. In the United States milk is fortified with 400 IU per litre while Germany adds 750–1000 IU of vitamin D per litre. Vitamin D in food is quite stable, and it is not lost through storage, processing or cooking. Fish liver oils are very rich sources of vitamins D and A, and the use of fish liver oils to cure deficiency diseases was first carried out in 1918. In bright sunlight, the skin can produce up to 10 IU of vitamin D_3 per square centimetre of skin, depending on the level of pigment in the skin. Dark skin allows less ultraviolet light to reach the deeper layers of the skin and so less vitamin D is produced. Air pollution, which absorbs ultraviolet light, can also reduce the penetration of ultraviolet rays into the skin and lessen the level of vitamin D produced. Like vitamin A, the recommended requirements for vitamin D are set in IU. Supplements of 1000 IU per day are recommended for infants between two weeks and two years of age. Then from two years to fifteen years, supplements of 500–1000 IU should be given daily. The adult RDA is around 400 IU, while nursing mothers are recommended to consume between 400 and 800 IU daily. Supplements of vitamin D are generally required only in the dark winter months, particularly for children and elderly people.

Humans absorb vitamin D through the small intestine, with bile involved in the process. Hence diseases of the pancreas, liver, gall bladder or intestines can reduce vitamin D absorption, as can disruption to the absorption of fats or anti-epilepsy medication. Monitoring the level of vitamin D in the body can be done by analysing blood serum, as vitamin D binds itself to certain blood proteins. The form produced is 25–dihydroxycholecalciferol, and this is produced in the liver from calciferol. Vitamin D has various effects on the body. It acts like a hormone and has effects on distant areas of the body. The vitamin acts on the body to aid the absorption of calcium and phosphorus from the ileum into the blood, which are then used in the formation and strengthening of bones and teeth. Deleterious effects can occur with large doses of vitamin D, as if too much phosphorus and calcium are present in the blood, the bones and teeth can become over-calcified, calculus stones may form in the kidneys and other organs, and hardening of the arteries, because of calcium deposits, may occur. If supplement intake is in excess of 50,000 IU daily, there is a risk of overdose, and by taking 25,000 IU daily over a long period, poisoning can occur. Symptoms of this extreme intake are general discomfort, itchy eyes and skin, unquenchable thirst, and frequent diarrhoea. Also, tests would show calcium build-up in the blood vessels, liver, lungs and kidneys. Because of these severe symptoms and the risk of overdose, adults should take only around 400 IU per day. The other role of vitamin D is to regulate the permeability of cell membranes.

Deficiency of vitamin D causes rickets in children, with irregular growth and softening of the bones. It can also lead to distorted limbs, swollen joints and deformities of the chest. Rickets is still seen in children of some developing countries but is rare in the industrialized world. A similar disease called osteomalacia occurs in adults, where calcium is lost from the bone matrix, making it soft with accompanying weakness, fracture, pain and weight loss. This may be particularly common during pregnancy. In children, vitamin D is essential to the normal development of teeth, and lack of vitamin D can give rise to dental caries. In both children and adults, lack of vitamin D and reduced levels of calcium in the blood may prompt muscle weakness and cramp, as the calcium is needed for correct contraction and relaxation of both smooth muscle and cardiac muscle tissue. With extended periods of vitamin D deficiency, which has led to reduced calcium absorption, a disease called osteoporosis can occur. Here the body reabsorbs existing bone so that the quantity of bone mass is reduced. It causes pain, particularly in the lower back, with loss of stature and an increased risk of fractures. The disease may occur naturally in post-menopausal women, in immobilized patients, in long-term steroid treatments and because of extreme vitamin D/calcium deficiency.

vitamin E

tocopherols–alpha, beta, gamma and delta (a, ß, _ and ∂) forms

This vitamin is actually a group of closely related compounds, all of which have vitamin E activity. They are fat-soluble, and the strongest and most commonly used chemical is alpha-tocopherol. They cannot be produced in the human body, and we depend entirely on our dietary intake. Good sources of vitamin E are wheat germ, soya bean, cotton seed, corn and peanut oils, margarine, raw seeds and nuts, eggs, butter, sweet potatoes, liver and some green-leaved vegetables. Unfortunately, much of the vitamin E in foodstuffs is lost because of contact with the air, processing, preserving and deep-freezing. Vitamin E was first discovered in 1923, when experiments on rats showed that a lack of vitamin E caused infertility in male rats and an increased risk of miscarriage in female rats. Further study found that similar reproductive problems arose in other vertebrate groups, along with kidney degeneration and other wasting symptoms.

The role of vitamin E in the body includes being essential for muscle development, and it is important in making red blood cells resistant to haemolysis or breakdown. It may also be essential for normal reproductive function in both sexes, but the precise mechanism for this process is as yet unknown. The most important action vitamin E has is as a lipid-soluble antioxidant that protects highly unsaturated fatty acids in cell membranes from attack by free radicals and peroxides. It acts inside the cell to maintain the stability of polyunsaturated fatty acids and similar fat-like compounds, such as hormones from the pituitary, adrenal and sex glands, as well as vitamin A. The antioxidant properties of vitamin E are enhanced by the enzyme glutathione peroxidase, which contains selenium. Vitamin C is also important in prolonging and reinforcing the beneficial effects of vitamin E.

As an antioxidant, vitamin E has recently shown that, in connection with selenium, it can prevent cancer in experimental animals. Further research has told us that vitamin E may be of use as a prophylactic drug for cancer in humans and can also help patients undergoing radiotherapy or chemotherapy withstand the treatment, with less harmful side effects. Indeed, blood serum values of vitamin E of less than 18 μmol l^{-1} have been shown to suggest an increased risk of cancer. Another area of interest is that of cardiovascular diseases and blood clots, and how vitamin E can help these conditions. How vitamin E works in the body would seem to be connected to prostaglandins, but research into this link has only just started. High doses of vitamin E are known to stop the aggregation of blood platelets and so help prevent blood clots or thromboses forming. At megadoses greater than 800mg per day, vitamin E acts as an anticoagulant that prevents or delays blood clotting. Since the 1940s vitamin E has been used for correcting cardiovascular disorders like *claudicatio intermittens* (window-watcher's disease). This disease causes sufferers to struggle to walk even short distances because of a circulatory disorder in the legs, and many patients found supplements of vitamin E very helpful. The only drawback is that it may take several to many months for a beneficial effect to arise.

Patients with coronary heart disease who are treated with vitamin E show conflicting results Some studies in the early days of vitamin E treatment showed very good results, but more recent research has been disappointing. Vitamin E influences the development and functioning of the smooth and striped muscles, and is able to prevent muscle degeneration. It is particularly good for cardiac muscles. However, a new water-soluble analogue of vitamin E has been manufactured, and this has been shown in animal studies to have a good protective effect on the heart. Best results are obtained with the new vitamin E analogue, selenium and vitamin E itself. Like vitamins A, B_5, B_6 and C, vitamin E improves the activity of the immune system and so strengthens resistance to diseases, including those of a bacterial or viral nature. In order for this to occur, supplements in the range of 5–20mg per kilogram of body weight are required, which works out at 350–1400mg for a person weighing 70kg (154lbs). Vitamin E also acts to prevent cataract formation, when daily doses of 300–400mg are taken. This effect is reinforced by beta-carotene and vitamin C. This vitamin also protects against overdoses of selenium and digoxin, a heart stimulant obtained from the foxglove plant. Vitamin E may also have detoxifying effects on the side effects of cytostatic drugs like adriamycin and may detoxify harmful heavy metals such as cadmium.

One of the most promising areas of vitamin E therapy is in Parkinson's disease, which is a progressive, degenerative, neurological disorder caused by damage in the cerebral ganglia and lack of neurotransmitters. It is more common in men, normally developing in people over sixty, and with no known cure. Most treatments try to keep the condition under control but with limited success. Ongoing research in Canada and the United States has shown that the disease may occur because of the action of free radicals, suggesting that antioxidants may be of benefit in preventing the illness in the first place. This study has also shown that doses of 300mg of vitamin C and of 400–3200mg of vitamin E per day could slow down the progress of the disease. Indeed, antioxidant vitamin therapy could delay the requirement for traditional Parkinson's medicines such as levo-dopa. These large daily doses of vitamin C and E caused no problems with no signs of toxicity. Vitamin E is also recommended for heart patients with angina pectoris or recent heart attack patients at a dose of 400mg each day, often in association with other antioxidants and selenium. Doses of up to 1000mg per day are used to prevent new blood clots and to improve the heart muscle's resistance to oxygen deficiency. This vitamin is important for women as it can be taken during pregnancy and when breastfeeding with no risk of harm to the baby. Vitamin E is vital for both male and female fertility and prevents miscarriage of the foetus as it promotes the normal development of the foetus in the womb and ensures a normal pregnancy without complications. Vitamin E may also be given as a therapy in rheumatism and at the menopause. Unfortunately, attempts to use vitamin E to help some muscle diseases and muscular dystrophy have not had many beneficial results. Elderly people can benefit from supplements of vitamin E and selenium. Studies in Germany and Finland have shown that 400mg of vitamin E per day results in a significant improvement in the psychological and physical health of elderly people.

Like the other fat-soluble vitamins, vitamin E is stored in the body, but there is no risk of overdosing. Studies completed in Canada have shown that doses of up to 10g of vitamin E per day over an extended time gave rise to no ill effects. Some people, however, taking doses of 1000mg and more a day may develop stomach problems and diarrhoea.

vitamin H

biotin

Debate continues as to whether biotin is classified as a vitamin or as one of the B complex vitamins. Biotin was identified in 1940 by Albert Szent-Györgyi, Vincent Du Vigneaud and co-workers. It is water-soluble, crystalline and lacking in colour when isolated. The vitamin is found in liver, kidney, egg yolk, yeast, oats, nuts, milk chocolate and most vegetables. It is also produced naturally by intestinal bacteria, and this normally covers most of our daily requirements. Deficiency may result if a person consumes large quantities of raw egg white. The egg white contains a glycoprotein, called avidin, that forms a complex with biotin that cannot be broken down by the digestive enzymes. This only really occurs if around 20 raw egg whites are consumed per day, and this is fairly uncommon today.

Biotin is an active compound that participates in many enzymatic reactions. It serves as a prosthetic group on the enzyme, which fixes carbon dioxide into an organic compound. This occurs in intermediate compounds in the Krebs cycle, which produces energy from dietary glucose. Biotin is also known as a co-enzyme in the synthesis of fatty acids and purines in the body. Unusually, biotin is also involved in gluconeogenesis, a process in which glucose is produced from non-carbohydrate sources, e.g. amino acids. This occurs only when the diet contains insufficient carbohydrate for energy needs. Biotin also contributes to the production of antibodies and increases the effectiveness of the immune system.

Deficiency of biotin can occur and produces symptoms of loss of appetite, infections of the mucous membranes, depression, insomnia, muscle pains, rashes, discomfort and increased levels of cholesterol in the blood. These problems can be cleared up easily by daily injections of 150–300μg of biotin. Elderly people, athletes and people with epilepsy are known to have relatively low levels of biotin in their blood. Children may be affected by two skin diseases that have been linked to biotin deficiency. Leiner's disease is a widespread form of seborrhoeic eczema linked to lack of biotin, while the other is a more serious fungoid infection. This infection affects the growth of hair and causes disorders of both the central nervous system and the immune system. This all stems from a malfunction of the carboxylase enzyme, which requires biotin to function effectively, and it is resolved within a few days of biotin supplementation. Fortunately, both diseases are exceedingly rare.

Biotin has been tried as part of a therapy to stop hair loss. Combinations of 200–400μg of biotin, para-aminobenzoic acid (PABA), inositol, minerals and essential fatty acids have been tried with variable success.

vitamin K

K_1—phytomenadione, K_2_menaquinane, K_3—menadione

Vitamin K is a fat-soluble vitamin that exists in three forms. Vitamin K_1 is a yellow substance that is produced naturally in plants but has also been made artificially. Vitamin K_2 is a slightly less active form of compound with a pale yellow colour and a more unsaturated structure than K_1. It is synthesized by various microorganisms that live in the gastrointestinal tract in humans. Vitamin K_3 (menadione) is of synthetic origin and is of much less importance than the other forms. Vitamins K_4 and K_5 are also produced artificially. They have twice the biological effects of natural vitamin K (K_1 or K_2). Vitamin K, like vitamin E, exists as a group of similar chemicals, called quinones, which are essential for human health. Much of the vitamin K requirement is covered by the vitamin K_2 produced by the intestinal bacteria. It is found in green vegetables, especially brassica species, seaweed, potatoes, liver, eggs, wheat germ, fish, nuts, alfalfa, molasses, yoghurt, fish liver oils, dairy products, corn and soya bean oils.

Vitamin K was discovered in 1935 by Henrik Dam, when he found that a mixture of alfalfa and putrefying fish powder could prevent haemorrhaging in chickens fed on a low-fat diet. The chemical isolated from alfalfa was phytomenadione—K_1. Vitamin K is resistant to heat, air and damp conditions, but the chemicals quickly decompose on exposure to sunlight or ultraviolet light. Like other fat-soluble vitamins, vitamin K is absorbed with fat in the intestines and then moves into the bloodstream via the lymphatic system.

The role of vitamin K in the body appears to be in allowing the synthesis of coagulation factors such as prothrombin in the liver. Prothrombin is found free in the blood and is the inactive precursor to thrombin itself. Thrombin is an enzyme coagulation factor that converts the soluble protein fibrinogen into the insoluble protein fibrin at the last stage of blood-clotting. Vitamin K is involved in the production of a number of coagulation factors, which, like prothrombin, undertake a series of reactions that turn blood from a liquid to a solid state, reducing blood loss and sealing the wound so that it may heal more successfully. Some sources believe that vitamin K is also involved in the electron transport chain and oxidative phosphorylation; two components of energy metabolism.

Deficiency in phytomenadione (vitamin K_1) may lead to the onset of osteoporosis or brittle bone disease. Vitamin K_1 is the catalyst for the metabolism of osteocalcin, which makes up the protein matrix for new bone formation. As long as vitamin K_1 is present, osteocalcin will bind calcium ions, and the bones will undergo calcification as normal. Many bone specialists now recommend monitoring the blood serum level of vitamin K_1 to check women at risk from osteoporosis and to try to prevent the disease starting. If osteoporosis is already affecting a woman's bones, then supplements of vitamin K_1 would give a better chance of recalcifying her bone tissues with fewer problems of pain, fractures or loss of stature. Blood serum testing is now recommended for women with the disease and women whose family history shows osteoporosis. This testing may not be possible in people on anticoagulant therapy after blood clotting or thrombosis problems. Deficiency in vitamin K_1 normally arises in people who do not eat enough green vegetables and in people whose digestion and absorption of fats is impaired. Studies in Japan have shown that supplements of vitamin K_1 in osteoporotic women reduced the calcium loss from their bones from 18 to 50 per cent and that vitamin K_1 supplements resulted in faster healing of bone fractures, both in normal and osteoporotic individuals.

Deficiency of vitamin K can occur because of alcoholism, liver and intestinal diseases and in disturbances to fat absorption in the digestive system. Long-term antibiotic use may suppress the natural bacterial flora of the gastrointestinal tract producing vitamin K, so there is a risk of internal bleeding as the blood lacks the necessary coagulation factors.

Aspirin-containing painkillers also increase the body's requirement for vitamin K. Vitamin K is also given to patients before some types of major surgery, and it has been confirmed that large doses (more than 800mg) of vitamin E has an anticoagulant property that interferes with the addition of vitamin K. Supplements of vitamin K are generally given only as a preventative treatment to people at risk from osteoporosis, to osteoporotic people, to people with livers damaged by alcohol, or to people with severe burns who are treated with antibiotics. Newborn babies are given injections of vitamin K to prevent haemorrhage, as they do not have intestinal bacteria that produce it naturally until a few days after birth. People should consult their doctor before starting supplements of vitamin K, and some people with liver diseases cannot tolerate the action of the vitamin. There is no official RDA for vitamin K, but most adults require at least 1mg per day.

vitamin P

bioflavinoids, rutin, citrin, hesperidin

This name is given to a group of naturally occurring coloured pigments that are produced by plants. They are generally found in citrus fruits or vegetables as orange or yellow pigments. Bioflavinoids are found in carrots, rosehips, plums, oranges, lemons, etc, and the human requirement is thought to be very small. Bioflavinoids may be found as crystalline structures or as flavone glycosides in plants, depending on the type of bioflavinoid. They act in the body to strengthen the walls of blood capillaries and so prevent purpura, or bleeding into the tissues. Bioflavinoids are also known to be essential for the absorption and metabolism of vitamin C in the body. Supplements of bioflavinoids are taken by athletes, as they are suggested to heal pulled muscles faster and speed healing of sprained joints and chafed skin. Bioflavinoids may also be of benefit in treating hypertension (high blood pressure) and in reinforcing the beneficial effects of vitamin C on the connective tissues. Rutin ($C_{27}H_{30}O_{16}$, $3H_2O$) is a crystalline bioflavinoid found in buckwheat, which acts as an antioxidant. It is very well thought of in Russia, where diet supplements of 1g of rutin is given each day as a protective measure.

Vitamin-like substances

carnitine

$(CH_3)_3 NCH_2 CH(OH) CH_2 COOH$

chemical name: alpha-hydroxy-gamma-butyo-betaine

This is a vitamin-like substance that is found in several tissues, including skeletal and heart muscle. It functions as a carrier molecule, moving fatty acids across the mitochondrial membrane inside cells. This allows biosynthesis of fatty acids or breakdown of the fatty acids to release energy. Carnitine can be synthesized in sufficient quantity in humans and higher animals, but its presence is required in the diet of some insects, including mealworms (*Tenebrio* species).

choline

$OHC_2H_4 N(CH_3)_3 OH$

chemical name: trimethyl-2-hydroxyethylammonium hydroxide

This is an alkaline compound that was first discovered in the 1930s. It was formerly classed as a B complex vitamin but is now termed a vitamin-like substance. It is found in wheat bran, egg yolk, brewer's yeast and offal, and only around 500mg of choline is required per day. This level is normally covered in vegetables, milk or lecithin intake. Choline is a constituent of a number of phospholipids, including lecithin (phosphatidylcholine), and also part of the neurotransmitter acetylcholine. For choline to be produced in humans requires an adequate supply of vitamin B_{12} (cyanocobalamin), vitamin B_9 (folic acid) and the amino acid methionine. It is still an essential vitamin for some animals and microorganisms.

Choline is involved in the synthesis of phospholipids, which form part of all lipid membranes, and is also involved with the transport of fats through the body. It is also essential for the metabolism of fats in humans and, apart from methionine, is the only substance known to take part in methylating reactions in the metabolism. It has been suggested that choline may reduce high levels of cholesterol in the blood, and it is possible that choline can pass over the blood brain barrier. Some studies indicate that it can improve the memory, but these claims have not been conclusively proven.

Deficiencies of choline in experiments with animals have caused fatty liver and cirrhosis of the liver, along with increased cholesterol levels, higher blood pressure and kidney damage. These results have not been repeated for humans. Choline deficiency has been linked to arteriosclerosis and even Alzheimer's disease, where rapid ageing of the brain tissue occurs and the patient becomes prematurely senile.

Supplementation of the diet with choline has no real basis, and some forms of choline may adversely affect the activity of intestinal bacteria, interrupting production of other vitamins.

inositol

$C_6H_{12}O_6$

chemical name: hexahydroxycyclohexane

This compound is an isomer of glucose, which exists in nine stereo-isomeric forms. The biologically active form is *meso* or *i*-inositor, which is widely distributed in plants and animals. Inositol is found in liver, wheat bran, maize (sweet corn), nuts, milk, brewer's yeast, oats, fruit, syrup, whole grains, cabbage, raisins, grapefruit, lecithin and peanuts. It is an essential vitamin and growth factor in some microorganisms and mice, but its exact function in the human body is unclear. Inositol was first isolated in the 1800s and is called a sugar alcohol because chemically it is an alcohol but its ring structure is similar to a sugar. In nature, inositol exists in at least four forms in compounds or complexes with salts or metals. Meso-inositol is absorbed into the body through the intestines, from where it moves to the heart, other muscles, the brain and other organs. Some of it is also used in the glucose metabolism. Meso-inositol also acts as the precursor to a phosphoglyceride, called phosphatidyl inositol, which forms an important part of the membranes, muscles and brain. Experiments on animals have shown that inositol has similar effects to choline in that it takes part in the construction of cell membranes and plasma lipoproteins, and inositol inhibits the accumulation of fat in the liver and other organs. Inositol is also found in the urine of diabetic people in higher levels than normal.

Deficiencies of inositol have been carried out experimentally in mice, where they show loss of hair, rashes, constipation, reduced growth and milk secretion, and congenital eye defects. These conditions could not be related to human deficiency of the compound.

para-aminobenzoic acid (PABA)

$C_7H_7NO_2$

other name: 4-aminobenzoic acid (PAB)

This substance exists as yellowish-red crystals and is a component of the folic acid (vitamin B_9) molecule. It was formerly included in the group of B complex vitamins. PABA is produced from intestinal bacteria in humans and can be detected in human urine, blood, sweat and spinal fluid. It is also contained in meat, cereals, eggs and milk. The chemical can prevent the hair of experimental animals turning grey, and can even restore normal hair colour if it has been caused by deficiencies of vitamin H (biotin), vitamin B_9 (folic acid) or vitamin B_5 (pantothenic acid). This process does not occur in humans. PABA is very similar in its chemical structure to drugs known as sulphonamides, which replace PABA in the processing reactions of bacteria, so preventing the bacteria from maturing and reproducing. So care should be taken as PABA can counteract treatment with sulphonamides and in lotions or creams as a sunscreen. PABA is nontoxic except in very large doses when it can lead to vomiting and discomfort.

ubiquinone, co-enzyme Q/co-enzyme Q10

structure $Q_{10} = C_9O_4H_9–C_{50}H_{90}$ chain

This chemical consists of a substituted benzoquinone with a long hydrocarbon chain. The number of repeated C_5H_9 units attached to the benzoquinone core varies from species to species, with yeasts having six or seven units (co-enzyme Q_6 or Q_7), some bacteria having eight (co-enzyme Q_8), and humans having co-enzyme Q_{10} as the biologically active form. In humans, it is found in the heart muscle. Ubiquinone has an important role in the metabolism as it forms part of the electron transport chain in the mitochondria. Ubiquinone, along with the other eight chemicals that make up the electron transport chain, is embedded in the inner membrane of the mitochondrion where each chemical switches between a reduced and an oxidized state, and the whole process produces energy. Ubiquinone exists in the oxidized quinone and the reduced quinol form when it has been given electrons or hydrogen from the flavoprotein above it in the chain.

Ubiquinone also acts as an antioxidant in cells and is of particular benefit in protecting heart patients from reperfusion injury. It is given to many heart patients as a protective measure. In Japan, ubiquinone is registered as a medicine.

lecithin

phosphatidylcholine

This substance belongs to a group called phospholipids, which are essential for the formation of cell membranes. Lecithin has developed into a popular food supplement in recent years, and it is found in soya beans and vegetable oils. It is also produced naturally in the human body as it forms part of bile, the digestive liquid that helps to break down fats in our diet. Lecithin has a specific role that helps to make cholesterol soluble. The phosphoglyceride is found in all animal and vegetable cells, both in the cell membranes and in the motochondrial membranes. Indeed, 40 per cent of brain tissue is made of phosphatidyl choline, which is a form of lecithin. Lecithin contains both choline and inositol in its structure, and this explains its large role in fat metabolism. Lecithin is also present in the lung surfactant, found in foetal and newborn lung tissue, that stops the walls of the lungs sticking together and collapsing. Several studies into the potential health benefits of lecithin have been carried out, and some people believe that lecithin may be able to decrease cholesterol levels and therefore reduce the risk of arteriosclerosis, ischaemic heart disease and blood clots. Similar research programmes have discovered that lecithin may improve the mental wellbeing and memory of elderly people as well as benefiting patients suffering from Alzheimer's disease, myasthenia gravis and Friedrich's ataxia.

lipoic acid

$C_8S_2H_{14}O_2$

This chemical was formerly classified as a B complex vitamin. It is required for the growth of a number of microorganisms species, but it is synthesized in sufficient quantities in the human body so that no intake from the diet is required. The structure is of a fatty acid chain joined by a disulphide bridge. Its function is to help carry out enzyme reactions that catalyse the removal of carbon dioxide groups from certain compounds in the Krebs cycle. This allows the maximum energy to be obtained from each molecule of glucose eaten.

Macrominerals

more than 100mg daily requirement

calcium

chemical symbol: Ca

Calcium is a metal that is widely distributed in nature as carbonate, sulphate, silicate and halide salts. It is found in milk, dairy products, hard tap water, fish (especially sardines and pilchards), white flour, bread, green leafy vegetables and fortified cereals. The mineral is absorbed into our bodies through the intestinal walls, and this process is facilitated by the presence of vitamin D. It is also influenced by the presence of stomach acids and by the intake of dietary fibre and proteins. Calcium also allows uptake of vitamin B_{12} (cyanocobalamin) from the intestines. The recommended dietary allowance for calcium varies between 500mg and 1000mg for healthy adults, with pregnant women requiring 1200mg and women over forty-five being encouraged to take 1500mg per day. There is a wide variety of recommended intake, and some sources state that pregnant women do not need higher levels of calcium as a woman's body absorbs many nutrients better while pregnant. The higher doses recommended for older women are to try to prevent osteoporosis, which is most common in post-menopausal women.

The human body contains large quantities of calcium—generally around 1200g, of which 99 per cent is found in the bones and teeth. Adequate levels of calcium are critical for babies and children while their teeth and bones are growing. Calcium is needed for the transmission of nerve impulses, maintaining the fluid balance and for muscle contraction. It is also important in the coagulation of blood, for cardiac activity and for the secretion of breast milk. Calcium is contained in soft tissue cells and in extracellular fluid where, if levels become elevated, it can trigger muscle weakness, lethargy and even coma. Even small deviations from the normal mineral concentration can cause influx of calcium into the cells, leading to cell damage or death, and prompting seizures. Calcium levels in the blood are generally $100mg/l^{-1}$ and are controlled by a combination of two hormones—thyrocalcitonin, which lowers the levels of calcium and phosphorus in the blood, and parathyroid hormone, which controls the distribution of calcium in the body between the blood and the bones. The amount of calcium in the bones and teeth is not static. There is actually a dynamic system in which calcium is taken away from the bone and replaced each day, showing that skeletal bone is a living tissue with an active metabolism. Any excess calcium may be deposited in the body as calculi, particularly in the kidney or bladder, as tartar on the teeth, or it is excreted via urine, faeces or sweat.

Deficiencies of calcium are rare but can occur because of a lack of vitamin D or a problem with calcium absorption in the intestines. Conditions caused by such a deficiency include rickets in children, with weakened development of bone mass and teeth. The adult form of rickets is called osteomalacia. Rickets in early life may predispose someone to develop osteoporosis in later life. Problems with the levels of calcium in the blood serum can develop because of a tumour affecting the parathyroid glands. Too little calcium intake weakens the bones, teeth, hair and nails and may also lead to allergic reactions developing. Calcium competes with magnesium in the body, and they need to be present in the correct proportions for both to function correctly. Magnesium can reduce high blood levels of calcium, but calcium can also help solve potassium deficiencies. Thus, many of the minerals and trace elements required are interdependent upon the presence of others. Therapeutic supplements of both calcium and magnesium have been used to treat joint problems and are also helpful for osteoporosis. This is the most difficult condition of calcium disorders to treat, and attempts have been made to relieve the disease using combinations of calcium, oestrogen, fluorine, magnesium, silicon and sex hormones. Injections of thyrocalcitonin have proved of some benefit, while fluorine is included to encourage bone growth and reduce the chance of fractures. Results have been mixed, but it has been discovered that calcium requires the presence of both magnesium and silicon for assimilation into the bones. For osteoporosis, prevention is better than cure, and the aim now is to ensure adequate intake of calcium in young women and teenagers as this may be the critical period that decides a person's susceptibility to the disease.

chlorine

chemical symbol: Cl

Chlorine is a trace element that is essential to the formation of digestive stomach acids, e.g. hydrochloric acid, HCl. It is also required for the correct functioning of the carbon dioxide transport system in the blood. When CO_2 bound by the red blood cells reaches the lungs, it can only be released and expelled out of the lungs if the procedure is triggered by the movement of chloride ions through a transmembrane protein found in red blood cells. The transmembrane protein is called the Band III protein, and it is found in the red blood cells of humans, rabbits, rats, salmon and trout, among other species. Chlorine is also very closely linked to sodium, and these elements regulate the acid-base balance, the fluid balance and the osmotic pressure in the blood. In excess of 100mg of chlorine is required per day, but there is generally too much chlorine in our diets in the form of table salt. The human body contains around 75g of chlorine, 60g of which is found in the blood plasma and tissue fluids.

magnesium

chemical symbol: Mg

Like calcium, magnesium is a metallic element that is found in the intracellular fluids of the body. Around 20–28g of magnesium is contained in the human body of an adult, 99 per cent of which is held within the cells. Most of that magnesium is in the bones or muscles, while only 1 per cent is found in the intracellular fluid or blood serum. This explains why analysis of blood serum does not give representative measurement for magnesium levels in the tissues. The RDA for this mineral is around 300mg, with pregnant women and nursing mothers requiring 450mg per day. Good sources of magnesium include green vegetables, wholemeal flour, milk, eggs, fish, pulses, shellfish, nuts (especially peanuts), meat, and cereals and their products. Absorption of the mineral into the bloodstream occurs via the intestines, and this uptake is highly variable. Generally around 30–40 per cent of the magnesium available is taken up, and when less magnesium is available, the percentage absorption increases. Absorption is deleteriously affected by dietary intake of calcium, phosphorus, proteins, saturated animal fat and fibre. The balance of magnesium in humans relates to the level of magnesium in the urine, and this is normally between 100 and 150mg per day. Higher levels of magnesium in the blood serum correlate to an increase in the level of magnesium eliminated via the urine. This process appears to be linked to calcium and sodium loss in the urine. In the body, magnesium is essential for the production and activation of many enzymes that regulate the metabolism of proteins, carbohydrates, lipids, nucleic acids and nucleotides (*see* Krebs cycle in the Glossary). Magnesium acts as a co-factor for approximately 90 enzymes in energy metabolism.

It is required to allow proper functioning of neurochemical transmissions and is vital for normal muscle function. In the cell it is vital for cell division and for all reactions with phosphates. If cells are deficient in magnesium, the permeability of the cell membranes changes, causing potassium and magnesium to be lost and replaced by sodium and calcium. This ultimately gives rise to a substance called AMP (adenosine monophosphate) that eventually leads to cell death. Magnesium is also needed for healthy bones and teeth and proper nerve function, and it allows vitamins B (thiamin) and

B_{12} (cyanocobalamin) to carry out their proper roles in the body. Magnesium acts on the heart muscle and the whole circulatory system as it prevents an increase in blood pressure. A deficiency of magnesium seems to lead to muscle weakness and fatigue and possible development of cardiac arrhythmia. A lack of the mineral is often see in heart patients and also increases the sensitivity of the heart to digoxin, a common cardiac remedy. Too little magnesium may cause nephrocalcinosis, where calcium deposits form in the kidney tissue, and this can be prevented by magnesium supplementation. Additional magnesium can also reduce the risk of occurrence of myocardial infarction, where a coronary artery becomes blocked, and it also reduces the chances of a second infarction occurring later in life. Around the turn of the century, the daily intake was around 1200mg (between three and four times today's RDA). A study of postmortems carried out at that time showed that out of 1000 individuals, none had died from a heart infarction.

This mineral also plays a role in both the cell and antibody-mediated immune response. If the diets of experimental animals are lacking in magnesium, then the levels of immunoglobulin antibodies is reduced by up to 60 per cent. The effect is especially strong for IgG, but the levels of IgA, IgE and IgM also fall. This process may occur because B-lymphocytes cannot develop into the antibody-producing plasma cells, and magnesium is suggested to be involved in that process in some manner. Further research is being carried out to determine the immunological properties of magnesium. The cell-mediated response consists of T-lymphocytes that require magnesium and calcium for proper maturation. Studies on rats have proved a direct link between magnesium deficiencies and impaired immune defence against allergic reactions and cancers, particularly lymphoma and leukaemia. Up to this point, no large human population studies have been carried out to consider a possible link between magnesium deficiency and disorders of the immune system. Magnesium deficiency in humans can occur because of a low dietary intake, problems with magnesium absorption in the intestines or because of excessive elimination of magnesium in the urine. Certain diseases can increase the level of magnesium lost, e.g. diabetes, kidney diseases and some hormonal disorders. Some drugs, such as diuretic medicines, and alcohol can increase the level of magnesium lost in the urine. A deficiency of magnesium is often accompanied with a lack of potassium, but this may not be easily detected by measuring blood serum only. Measurement of magnesium in the body via the blood cells, platelets or whole blood is far more accurate, but the best results are obtained by measuring magnesium loss through the urine over a 24-hour period. Magnesium deficiency can arise gradually over time, leading to symptoms of anxiety, fatigue, loss of appetite, hormonal disorders, nausea, insomnia, hypoglycaemia, muscle weakness and muscle cramps, and trembling ('restless legs'). A reduced level of magnesium in the body may also be linked to premenstrual tension. A serious deficiency of magnesium can, as mentioned before, lead to arrhythmia, which can be detected on an electrocardiogram (ECG).

This link between magnesium and heart problems has been studied since the 1960s, when it was found that there is a reduced incidence of heart disease in areas with hard water. Hard water contains calcium and magnesium, and this may supplement the dietary supply of these minerals. Thus, supplementation of the diet with magnesium may benefit a range of heart problems. This process does not harm the body, has a low cost and yet can reduce the damage after heart infarction and decreases the risk of fatal cardiac arrhythmia. Investigations in Denmark and Finland have shown that magnesium deficiency in the blood exists prior to a heart attack, and supplement therapy can reduce the risk of a repeated attack. Magnesium deficiency is also seen in cases of allergy or asthma that have been successfully treated with supplements. The mineral supplements seem to reduce the levels of histamine in the blood and allow the patient's condition to improve. Magnesium has an antihistamine effect and can alleviate the symptoms of many asthmatic patients or those with atopic eczema. Magnesium also is a mild tranquillizer and can replace tranquillizing medicines to some degree. Finally, the physical and psychological symptoms associated with undefined fatigue can be treated successfully with magnesium supplement.

Recent work has found a possible connection between breast cancer and blood levels of magnesium. This has yet to be substantiated, but it may be probable that low magnesium levels can predispose a person to developing cancer. At a conference in the United States, evidence was shown of correlations between insufficient magnesium intake and the onset of high blood pressure, cardiovascular diseases and complications in pregnancy. Many research workers now believe that 80 per cent of the United States population gets less than the recommended dietary intake of magnesium. Those most at risk are people who take diuretic or antibiotic drugs or heart medicines, which interfere with the normal metabolism of magnesium, and people who consume excessive amounts of alcohol. Some reports state that magnesium deficiency during pregnancy could result in migraines and in pregnancy-related high blood pressure. Miscarriage, stillbirths and low-birth-weight babies may be linked to inadequate supplies of magnesium. In animal experiments, supplementation with magnesium was said to reduce high blood pressure and limit the impact of arteriosclerosis in animals on a high cholesterol diet. Whether such actions can translate to humans remains to be seen.

phosphorus

chemical symbol: P

This is a nonmetallic element that is found in nature as phosphate salts. It is found in nearly all foodstuffs but particularly in high protein foods such as meat, dairy products, pulses and milk as well as most fruits and leafy green vegetables. The RDA for the mineral is 800mg for healthy adults and 1200mg for pregnant women and nursing mothers. Lack of phosphorus can cause weight loss, demineralization of bone, weakness, loss of appetite and stiff joints.

Other problems of phosphorus deficiency include anaemia, central nerve disorders and respiratory failure. A deficiency of phosphorus can affect bone density as it is required to form calcium phosphate, one of the main components of bone tissue. At the other extreme, too much phosphorus in the diet can interfere with absorption of calcium, iron, magnesium and zinc from the intestines.

Phosphorus is essential for many enzymes involved in glucose, protein and fat metabolism, e.g. phosphoglycerokinase in glycolysis. Phosphate also plays a part in adenosine triphosphate (ATP), which is vital throughout the energy production process, and in energy storage in humans. The majority of phosphorus is contained in the bones and teeth. Phosphorus is also essential to the formation of nucleic acids used in cell division.

potassium

chemical symbol: K

This is a metallic element that is required for the correct functioning of all plants and animals. It is found in most foods, including fresh fruits, vegetables (particularly potatoes), meat, milk, wholemeal flour, coffee, tea, cereals and their products, and salt substitutes. On average, a diet of 2800kcal contains 3–4g of potassium, and most people consume 2–4g per day. Somewhat surprisingly, around 15 per cent of our intake comes from coffee, which contains about 45mg of potassium per cup. The human body contains approximately 115–150g of the mineral, 98 per cent of which is held inside the cells. Potassium has an important role in the nervous system, the heart and the muscles. Its role is closely linked to that of sodium, as they have opposite effects. Potassium ions are the main alkaline ions found in the intracellular fluid and, along with sodium, it controls and maintains the electrical potential of the nervous system, which allows the transmission of nerve impulses out through the body. It helps regulate muscle contraction and neuromuscular excitability. Potassium also acts to maintain the body's osmotic balance and is also required by the heart muscle. A correct balance of potassium is needed to prevent arrhythmia. The mineral is also involved in several enzyme systems and in the metabolism of protein. Potassium uptake from the blood into the cells is possible only if magnesium is present, so supplementation of both minerals may be required to prevent any deficiency. Normal levels of potassium in the blood are between 3.5 and 5mmol/litre.

Potassium in the diet does not pose any risks to health in the same way that sodium does. Like many other minerals, potassium is absorbed through the intestines, and any excess is eliminated in the urine. If the intake is less than the level excreted, then potassium levels in the cells and blood serum will decrease. To replace these K^+ ions, the cells use H^+ ions or protons, which can cause problems by changing the cells' acidity. Increased loss of potassium in the urine can occur because of increased intake of alcohol, coffee and sugar. Diuretic drugs also increase the levels of potassium and magnesium lost, so treatment with these medicines should always be followed by checks of the potassium balance of the patient. Some diuretic drugs try to overcome this problem by retaining potassium in the body or by containing potassium themselves to supplement the intake. Symptoms of this mineral deficiency include muscle weakness, fatigue, fluid accumulation, 'pins and needles', loss of appetite, thirst, constipation, low blood pressure, and disorders of the kidneys and nervous systems. Inadequate potassium levels also affect the heart and change the way it is affected by some drugs, e.g. digitalis. It can lead to a higher risk of digitalis poisoning. Paralysis may result from insufficient potassium as the nerve impulses cannot be generated properly. Conversely, high levels of potassium in the blood can occur because of excessive fluid loss caused by prolonged vomiting or diarrhoea, producing symptoms of drowsiness, sensations of disorientation, weakness and cardiac problems including arrhythmia. This may finally lead to cardiac arrest. Excess potassium may occur because of kidney failure as the mineral cannot be eliminated effectively, and this can be shown on an electrocardiogram (ECG). Very high levels of potassium intake can reduce the effectiveness of anticoagulant medicines, and the dosage of such drugs may need to be raised during the summer when consumption of potassium-containing vegetables rises. Levels of potassium in the blood may be upset and reduced by diseases of the heart, liver and kidney, as well as by diabetes, cancer and hyperthyrosis, which is a hyperactive thyroid gland. Both too little and too much potassium can lead to metabolic disturbances.

Potassium supplements can be used to remedy several problems. Deficiency of the mineral because of diuretic drugs can be treated by giving a preventative dose of 1–2g daily or by administering 2–4g supplements per day, after checking the blood levels for potassium. This mineral may help reduce the accumulation of fluid in the body tissues, but this may not be advised during pregnancy. The source of the fluid retention should first be investigated before any treatment is given. In most cases where the swelling poses no threat to health, then potassium therapy may be safer than the use of diuretic drugs, which may deplete the body of minerals and vitamins. The excessive intake of coffee has diuretic properties and may cause deficiency in potassium despite the fact that coffee is a rich source of the mineral. Potassium tablets can cause problems as they may trigger stomach trouble or constipation, or irritate the mucous membranes. In susceptible people, such tablets may even trigger the development of a duodenal ulcer. They may also stick in the oesophagus unless taken with plenty of water. Some tablets are formulated to be slow-releasing, and they cause fewer side effects than the other tablets. Potassium supplementation is not tolerated well by patients with kidney failure.

Both potassium and magnesium deficiencies produce symptoms that are similar, and insufficient levels of one implies the other is also lacking. As mentioned before, both potassium and magnesium are required for uptake of potassium in the cells. If not, the blood serum values for potassium increases but not the cellular values. Calcium can correct symptoms caused by potassium deficiency but only to a certain extent.

sodium

chemical symbol: Na

Like potassium, sodium is a metal whose ions are the chief electrolyte in intracellular fluid. There is around 100g of sodium in the body, of which 50 per cent is found in the cells, primarily the bone cells. It is a major essential element for most animals, and humans require around 3g per day. We ingest sodium as sodium chloride, and it is added to many tinned, cured or processed foods, including cured meats, milk, smoked fish, bakery products, and tinned meat and vegetables. Most people use table salt, and as a consequence many people consume far too much salt, between 5 and 15g per day, or up to five times the recommended level. Around 50 per cent of our salt intake comes from preprocessed food, and 40 per cent is added at the table. Only 12 per cent of our intake actually comes from the sodium contained naturally in our food. Sodium may also be taken in by soft drinks, sodium-rich mineral waters or by headache tablets that contain acetyl salicylate (aspirin).

Sodium is critical to many processes in the body. Sodium ions are the main ions in intracellular fluid, and their interaction with potassium ions across cell membranes is required for survival. This process maintains the electrical potentials in the nervous system and permits normal functioning of nerves and muscles. The mineral is also involved with sustaining the acid-alkali balance, the production of adrenaline and the manufacturing of amino acids. Sodium also controls the water balance in the body.

The uptake of sodium from the small intestine and the stomach is easy, and the mineral goes on to be filtered from the bloodstream by the kidneys. Generally, over 90 per cent of sodium intake is eliminated from the body along with the urine. The main problem is excessive salt intake, which can raise blood pressure in people susceptible to this condition. High sodium levels can also aggravate or sustain already high blood pressure, and it may contribute to migraine attacks. It may also lead to a condition called hypernatraemia, which can cause fluid retention (oedema), mental confusion, seizures, and even coma. It can be treated by restoring the electrolyte balance in the body and may occur in bottle-fed babies as artificial milk has a much higher sodium content than breast milk. The babies cannot remove sodium from the body as efficiently as adults so dehydration may occur.

A deficiency of sodium is rare, but it may occur if sodium recycling is affected by a kidney malfunction. Sodium deficiency may arise if there is heavy sweat secretion because of a high workload or hot conditions. Symptoms of insufficient sodium include low blood pressure, weakness in the muscles, mild fever, respiratory problems, dizziness, loss of weight and general indisposition.

One of the prime reasons for hypertension, heart disorders and kidney complaints is excessive salt intake. Healthy salt habits should be taught in childhood as it becomes increasingly difficult to break our salt habits as we get older. Reduced intake of sodium may reduce our chances of developing high blood pressure in later life. We can replace sodium by the use of herbs, spices and herbal salt as seasonings and by using a salt substitute such as Pan-Salt or Lo-Salt, where some of the sodium chloride is replaced with potassium chloride to reduce our intake of sodium.

sulphur

chemical symbol: S

This is a yellow nonmetallic element that is required to form part of the amino acids cysteine and methionine. It is found in animal and vegetable proteins contained in meat, dairy products, pulses and nuts. There is no official RDA for this element, but it is essential for the formation of many proteins to make skin, nails and strong hair. Sulphur is also required for the proper development of cartilage and tendons, and it makes up part of many cell metabolites, such as co-enzyme A. Deficiency of sulphur is very rare and would occur only if there were insufficient intake of proteins that lack the amino acids that contain sulphur.

Microminerals

Fewer than 1mg–100mg daily requirement

bromine

chemical symbol: Br

Bromine would not seem to be required by the human body, although we take in between 1.5 and 2.5mg per day through our diets. Bromide salts of sodium, potassium and strontium are used in medicine as sedatives, hypnotics and analgesics. Their use dates back to the late 1880s, and bromides were formerly the standard treatment for epilepsy as they depress the activity of the central nervous system. They have largely been replaced by more recent anticonvulsant drugs but are still used occasionally in cases that will not respond to the new treatments. Bromides may be given in cases of insomnia, but the drug may produce a particular form of acne to erupt. Long-term use of bromides can lead to mental dullness, drowsiness, weakness, slurred speech, loss of sensation, and even coma. The problems can be rectified by immediate withdrawal of the drug.

chromium

chemical symbol: Cr

Chromium is a metallic element that is essential for normal body function. The amount of chromium required for health is unsure, but American authorities estimate that between 50 and 200µg is a safe and adequate dose. Chromium exists in an organic and inorganic form, with around 25 per cent of organic chromium being absorbed into the body against only 0.5 per cent of the inorganic form. Chromium is found in meat, unrefined and unprocessed foods, particularly wholemeal flour, cereals and cereal products, cheese, nuts, liver, brewer's yeast, fresh fruits, and herbs. Like most minerals, chromium is absorbed through the intestines and taken into the blood where it is bound by a protein called transferrin. After a period of time, chromium is released from the blood and stored in the liver, bone marrow and the spleen. In these tissues, chromium is found in association with vitamin B_3 (niacin). Absorption of chromium is inhibited by iron, manganese, zinc, titanium and calcium. Any excess of chromium is eliminated via the urine, and only a minute quantity is lost via the sweat or faeces. Like potassium and magnesium, the level of chromium in the blood serum or whole blood is tiny and does not reflect the chromium balance in the body. The only way to assess accurately the chromium balance is to measure the amounts of chromium excreted in the urine.

Chromium's role in the human body is not entirely clear, but it does seem to play a part in the functioning of skeletal muscles, helps in controlling the immune system and is involved in the metabolism and storage of sugars and fats. Animal studies have shown that lack of chromium causes reduced protein production, shorter life-span, eye damage and lowered fertility. Insufficient chromium in rats and monkeys has led to a decreased glucose tolerance, which can be resolved with supplements of the mineral. This link to glucose would also seem to occur in humans, and it has been suggested that chromium is part of the glucose tolerance factor molecule (GTF). This molecule is responsible for the foundation of a balance in sugar metabolism, but it has not yet been isolated. Recent studies have led doctors to believe that chromium is able to prevent hypoglycaemia, or low blood sugar levels. Conflicting results about this possibility have arisen, largely because of a lack of adequate control groups and variability in the preparations and dosage of chromium used.

Chromium deficiency may cause weakness, confusion, irritability and depression. It may also be a contributory factor in arteriosclerosis, as postmortem findings have shown that people with arteriosclerosis have very low values of chromium. Chromium values fall with advancing age in countries with higher levels of arteriosclerosis, in contrast to countries with little or no arteriosclerosis problem. Arteriosclerosis and heart disease are a particular problem in eastern Finland, for example, where the average daily intake of chromium is approximately 30µg and there are deficiencies in selenium also.

Some studies have proposed that organic chromium may be able to reduce the levels of fat in the blood. Further research is needed to shed some light on this possibility. Currently, chromium has no scientific basis for use as a therapy. Some nutritional doctors have prescribed chromium, either alone or with zinc and selenium, as therapy for people with coronary artery disease, diabetes, arrhythmia and hypoglycaemia. Several studies in Finland and Korea have shown that chromium supplements in diabetic patients can reduce the sugar levels in their blood, leading to less insulin requirement. Many patients have fewer symptoms and improved general health, and some people were able to stop taking insulin altogether. For chromium to regulate the sugar balance effectively requires a small quantity of insulin in the blood, so it works only in people who had a functioning pancreas, even if only to a small degree. The beneficial effects were also stopped if medicines that counteracted chromium were being taken. Chromium can also help patients with symptomatic hypoglycaemia, which causes headaches, anxiety, visual disturbances and general discomfort. Chromium is one of the minerals that warrants further study into its role in the human body.

cobalt

chemical symbol: Co

Cobalt is an essential trace element that forms part of the molecule of vitamin B_{12} (cyanocobalamin). It is found in meat, milk, eggs, green vegetables, figs and buckwheat. The human body contains about 1mg of cobalt, on average, and this is found in the muscles and bones. The role of cobalt in the body is as an essential component of vitamin B_{12}, and also it appears to stimulate the production of a glycoprotein hormone, called erythropoietin, when there is a lack of oxygen in the body. The reason for this action is unknown. Cobalt is taken into the body through the small intestines, and humans can tolerate quite large quantities of the mineral, side effects only arising if the daily intake is more than 20–30mg. The side effects can include a weakening of heart functioning and thyroid failure. There is no set RDA for this mineral as its role in humans is poorly understood. Deficiency of cobalt would result in insufficient vitamin B_{12}, which leads to weak muscles, bowel and nerve disorders, and pernicious anaemia. Some use of cobalt as a therapy in various types of anaemia has been attempted, as it has for reducing high blood pressure, but its use as a treatment has never been accepted.

An isotope of cobalt, Cobalt 60, is radioactive and has been used successfully to treat cancer with penetrating gamma-radiation.

copper

chemical symbol: Cu

Copper is an essential mineral that fulfils many roles in the body. There is about 80mg of copper inside the average human, most of it in the liver, brain, muscles, heart and the bones. The RDA for copper is between 2 and 5mg per day, and this comes from shellfish (particularly oysters), cocoa, tap water, liver, kidney, raisins, peas, nuts (particularly brazil nuts) and brewer's yeast. Copper is absorbed in both the stomach and the small intestine, and if the body reserves are full, then excess copper is excreted in the faeces and absorption drops by 80–90 per cent. Absorption is also affected by the presence of fibre or protein in the intestine as well as cadmium, iron, zinc, cobalt and molybdenum. Copper is particularly affected by zinc as the two minerals compete to form compounds with proteins. In the blood, copper is found in the red blood cells and the plasma. In the red blood cells, some of the copper is loosely attached to amino acids, and this reserve is called the labile pool or metabolic storage. Most of the copper in the red blood cells (60 per cent) is bound to the enzyme copper-zinc superoxide dismutase (CuZn SOD), which is called the stable pool or permanent storage. Currently, little is known about the copper metabolism or the movement of the copper reserves from pool to pool. This CuZn SOD enzyme contains two copper and two zinc atoms, and it protects the cells from free radicals and peroxides, especially superoxides that have a structure of O_2^- and are produced in respiration.

The copper held in the plasma is usually bound to a protein called ceruloplasmin. This protein is dark blue in colour, is produced in the liver and contains eight copper atoms. It acts as a natural antioxidant and is found in elevated levels during infection or inflammation when the body is exposed to excess free radicals. Ceruloplasmin also regulates the level of the hormones melatonin, adrenaline, noradrenaline and serotonin in the blood plasma. The protein is needed for the production of red blood cells as it stops storage of iron in the liver and directs it to the blood cells. Deficiency of copper, and so ceruloplasmin, causes easier oxidation of iron, and this may contribute to the production of superoxide radicals in cells. The levels of ceruloplasmin in the blood rise during physical activity.

The levels of copper in the blood are normally 90–145μgl^{-1} in plasma and 85–125μgl^{-1} in whole blood. This can change because of oestrogen treatment and pregnancy. Copper values rise during infection (because of the increased amounts of ceruloplasmin in the blood), and this can be used to gauge the activity of diseases such as arthritis.

As mentioned previously, copper has an active role in the superoxide dismutase (SOD) enzyme. The CuZn SOD enzyme is the fifth most common protein in the human organism and is found in the red blood cells and all tissues. Its job is to make oxygen-free radicals harmless to the cells in a similar way to the selenium enzyme glutathione peroxidase. Tests have been done to see if this enzyme can be used as a therapy for some diseases, e.g. inflamed joints in arthritis. Results showed a short-lasting but beneficial effect, and it was found that SOD was more effective in reducing the level of the rheumatoid factor than aspirin-type drugs. SOD was also seen to reduce the levels of PGE2, which is a harmful prostaglandin chemical. SOD has proved effective in easing osteoarthritis as well, and more studies should reveal the range of conditions this enzyme may help.

Another enzyme that requires copper is cytochrome oxidase, and it is absolutely critical for the metabolism. If copper is deficient then levels of the enzyme fall and energy production in the cells falls also. This has a large knock-on effect on the whole food metabolism of the body. Copper is found in two other enzymes—ascorbic acid oxidase and tyrosinases.

Copper deficiency is fairly rare but can result in serious diseases such as Menke's syndrome or Wilson's disease. Deficiency can result from problems with the absorption of food because of a biliary obstruction or an inflamed liver caused by biliary cirrhosis. Symptoms of insufficient copper include hair loss, changes in hair colour and texture, diarrhoea, anaemia, disturbances to the nervous system, low white blood cell count, and bone diseases. Inadequate copper intake in children can lead to brittle bones and inhibition of growth. Lack of copper can lead to an elevated risk of heart and circulatory complaints, particularly if it occurs with a deficiency of selenium. This would affect the activity of both major antioxidant enzymes, CuZn SOD and glutathione peroxidase, allowing free radicals to do much more cell damage. This problem is particularly bad for people with constricted blood vessels because oxygen deficiency (ischaemia) encourages the production of free radicals.

At the onset of an infection of any origin, the levels of ceruloplasmin and copper in the blood serum rise within a few hours. Amounts of zinc in the blood fall quickly at the same time as the copper levels rise when a person has an infectious disease such as tuberculosis of the lung. This means values of zinc and copper in the blood can be used as an indirect guide to hidden infections in some part of the body. In most cases, the levels of both minerals in the blood return to normal after a few weeks.

Copper levels in the blood are also affected by malignant tumours in the body. Cancers of the womb, lungs, breast and bladder cause increased copper in the blood, as does Hodgkin's disease and non-Hodgkin's lymphoma. Cancer of the prostate shows no changes in blood levels of copper. So elevated blood levels of the mineral should be investigated further, but they do not automatically mean that cancer is present in the body. Medicinal treatment of cancer returns copper levels to normal, and any rise in level thereafter may indicate a possible relapse of the disease.

fluorine

chemical symbol: F

Elemental fluorine exists as a gas, but it is used in the human body as fluoride salts. There is between 3 and 7mg of fluorine in the average adult and that normally comes from fluoridated drinking water, toothpastes, tea, cereals, meat and fish (especially sardines, herring and mackerel). The American RDA is from 1.0 to 4.0mg daily for healthy adults. Dietary fluoride is quickly and totally absorbed into the body, and fats can increase the level of absorption. Absorption is reduced by calcium, sodium chloride and aluminium. The fluoride is moved to the bones, teeth, kidneys, the aorta and other tissues via the blood. Levels of fluorine in soft tissues stay relatively constant over time, but levels in the bones increase with age. Excess fluoride is excreted in the urine, and it reflects both the level of intake and the previous intake of the mineral. Kidney complaints change or stop the level of fluorine loss.

The main role of fluoride is to be incorporated into tooth enamel, making the teeth more resistant to dental caries and attack by bacteria and plaque acids. Fluoride ions enter enamel as it is forming and also after teeth have erupted by absorption through the surfaces. There is some debate as to whether the addition of fluoride to the water is acceptable. Much of the evidence shows that water containing up to 1 part per million of fluoride results in reduced incidence of dental caries. Fluoridation of water would appear to be the easiest way to ensure the majority of the population receives enough fluoride. There is also some debate as to whether fluoride can strengthen the bones and prevent or slow down osteoporosis. Conflicting results have been found in studies from France, Finland and Denmark, where people were treated with fluoride to help osteoporosis. One of the Finnish studies thought that additional fluoride may increase the risk of breaking the femora or thigh bone. It has been agreed that fluorine, along with calcium and vitamin D, can increase the bone mass in osteoporotic patients. The new bone mass hardens but the tissue formed does not compare to normal bone composition.

Fluoride may have some link with the incidence of cardiovascular disease. Several studies have shown both an increased and decreased risk with fluoride intake, and these ambiguous results may be because of the variation in methods of study or external factors such as dietary habits, vitamin and mineral intake, the hardness of the water and the level of pollutants in the environment. Excessive intake of fluoride can cause problems, including fluorosis, a condition that results in discoloration and mottling of the teeth. Other problems may include calcification of the ligaments and increased density of the bones of the spine, pelvis and limbs.

Fluoride deficiency is uncommon in humans, but in animals it can cause limited growth, disorders in the development of teeth, and hair loss.

iodine

chemical symbol: I

Similar to fluorine, iodine is a gas in its simplest form but commonly forms iodide salts. The human body contains only 20–50μg of iodine, but it plays a critical role in the production of many hormones, and it is linked to proper growth and development. Iodine is found in iodized table salt, seafood including seaweed, meat, and fruit and vegetables in areas where the soil contains iodine. The average adult needs 100–200μg of iodine daily, and deficiencies can cause serious problems. Almost 80 per cent of the iodine found in the body is in the thyroid gland, where iodine is bound to the amino acid tyrosine. Iodine is used to produce the thyroid hormones thyroxine (T_4) and triiodothyronine (T_3). These hormones act to increase the metabolic rate, regulate carbohydrate, protein and fat catabolism, promote development of the central nervous system, and stimulate the synthesis of many other enzymes. They also sustain secretion of growth hormone, are necessary for muscle tone and vigour, and maintain the heart rate, its force and its output, as well as ensuring proper skeletal maturation. For a small gland, it plays a large role in development through childhood and then continuing through our adult lives. Iodine's role in the thyroid gland was first noticed in 1818. Dietary iodine is absorbed, and a third of it goes directly to the thyroid gland while the rest is eliminated in the urine. Unusually, the iodine that is lost also seems to have some effect on our bodies before elimination but what happens precisely is not yet known.

Deficiency of iodine can result in a drop in the metabolic rate, which causes fatigue, drowsiness, lethargy and weight gain. Reduced production of the thyroid hormones in pregnancy or in the early life of an infant can cause a disease called cretinism. The child suffers from dwarfism, mental retardation, and coarse facial features and skin. If the condition is detected early enough (within the first six weeks of life) then treatment with injections of thyroid hormones can significantly help the condition. Several countries have set up automatic biochemical screening programmes in order to trace cases of cretinism early.

The main problem of iodine deficiency is a disease called goitre. It occurs in four forms, but all result in swelling of the neck caused by enlargement of the thyroid gland. This occurs because of a lack of dietary iodine so the gland grows in order to produce more hormone (endemic goitre), because of simple excessive growth of the gland (sporadic goitre), or because of overactivity of the gland, sometimes caused by autoimmune diseases, such as in lymphadenoid goitre or Grave's disease (exothalmic goitre). Iodine deficiency was common in parts of Europe up to the 1940s and 1950s. Then iodine was added to table salt, increasing the dietary intake of iodine, and the problem was solved. Iodine deficiency still occurs in some areas of Africa, South America and Asia. Iodine tablets have been used to reduce the dangers of radioactive radiation in people who have been exposed to excessive radiation, e.g. people exposed to fallout or radiation from the Chernobyl disaster or some workers in the nuclear industry. Iodine isotopes that emit radioactivity are used in scanning procedures, e.g. of the gall bladder, and in treatment of some cancers. Iodine is widely used as a skin disinfectant.

iron

chemical symbol: Fe

Iron is a metallic element essential to life and many biological processes. The average adult has around 4g of iron in the body, 65 per cent in haemoglobin, 10 per cent in the myoglobin, while the rest is stored in the liver, kidneys, spleen, the bone marrow and other organs. The RDA for adults is 14–18mg and 30–60mg in pregnant women. Iron supplementation is given as the rule to breastfeeding women as well. Iron occurs in three forms, haem iron from meat, non-haem iron from vegetables, and non-haem iron added to foodstuffs. Each type is absorbed with differing degrees of difficulty, and absorption of any iron from the diet is generally poor, at around 5 per cent of the dietary intake. The best sources of iron are meat (especially liver), offal, blood, peas, parsley, pulses, eggs, whole grains, green leafy vegetables, nuts (particularly almonds), cocoa, apricots and figs, fortified white flour and products, and fortified breakfast cereals. In meat, 40 per cent of the meat is haem iron, and generally around 24 per cent of this is absorbed. This figure may seem low but actually reflects a good level of absorption. Haem-iron uptake is not affected by other dietary components. Non-haem iron is more difficult in uptake and generally is significantly affected by other substances in the diet. Coffee, tea and calcium all inhibit the absorption of iron, but it is increased by vitamin C. The calcium in milk, for example, competes with iron and makes it less available for uptake into the bloodstream. Wheat flour and some breakfast cereals are commonly fortified with iron. At first glance this may seem beneficial, but there is a range of formulations of iron that are added to the foodstuffs. Most countries add iron as ferrous iron powder that is absorbed pretty well without any interference from other foods. In Sweden, iron is added as ferric orthosulphate, which is taken up by the body particularly well. A problem may arise with the soluble ferrosulphate that is added to breast-milk substitutes, as it tends to react with the fats in the milk, leading to lipid peroxidation.

Iron is absorbed into the body through the upper section of the small intestine, changing from ferrous to ferric iron in the process. It then enters the blood, where most of the iron binds to the protein called transferrin. Some iron remains in the free state in the blood serum. The mineral then binds itself to the protein haemoglobin in the red blood cells. This procedure requires vitamin E, copper, cobalt and molybdenum to be present. Haemoglobin is the respiratory pigment found in the blood of all vertebrates, and it is composed of the haem group, composed of iron and porphyrin, a natural pigment, and the protein globin. Haemoglobin exists in two forms—oxyhaemoglobin, which is formed in the lungs and carries oxygen to all the body tissues, where it is reduced and the oxygen is released. This reduced haemoglobin is purplish in colour, compared to the scarlet of oxyhaemoglobin. As well as transporting oxygen, haemoglobin carries carbon dioxide to the lungs, where it is exhaled, and it helps regulate the acidity of the blood. Iron is also moved via the blood to the myoglobin found in the muscles. Myoglobin is similar to haemoglobin but smaller in size. It is used for oxygen production in the muscles during periods of oxygen deficiency and acts as an emergency oxygen store. Iron is also found in the cytochromes, which are protein-haem compounds important because they act as electron transfer agents in biological reactions. They are found associated with mitochondria inside cells and are very important in the electron transport chain. Iron is stored in an iron-protein complex, called ferritin, and in haemosiderin, which is a protein shell containing iron salts, both of which are stored in the tissues. As already mentioned, iron is needed for the production of red blood corpuscles and to transport oxygen round the body, and it also allows many enzymes to function well. Iron is also required for energy production in the cells. Iron is essential for the metabolism of all the B vitamins.

Deficiency of iron normally results from an unvaried diet, unhealthy eating habits, inadequate intake of vitamin C, and too little meat in the diet. Lack of iron results in anaemia, which is the most common nutritional deficiency disease in the industrialized world. Anaemia normally occurs because of a decreased capacity to absorb the mineral, caused by lack of vitamin C or the presence of inhibitory chemicals. Anaemia may be caused by heavy menstrual bleeding and haemorrhaging in the gastrointestinal tract because of cancer, stomach ulcers or haemorrhoids. Rheumatic complaints and long-term infections can also reduce the body's reserves of iron. Iron loss may be about 0.8–1.0mg per day in adults, but during menstruation women may lose around 1.4mg per day. Anaemia may also be caused by insufficient intake of vitamin B_9 (folic acid) or vitamin B_{12} (cyanocobalamin), which are necessary, along with iron, to form haemoglobin. Symptoms of anaemia include tiredness, pale skin, breathlessness, loss of strength, nervousness, feeling weak, fainting and palpitations. The haemoglobin content of the blood is normally 12–16g per 100ml, and if this falls below 12g per 100ml, a person is considered anaemic.

Other problems of iron deficiency include a weakening of the white blood cell defence system, which leaves an increased risk of contracting infectious diseases. Iron is also required for the proper functioning of the T-lymphocytes and for enabling them to identify virus, bacteria and cancer cells. Diet supplementation with iron can reduce the number of cases of anaemia and respiratory tract infections in children. Iron supplementation can show dramatic effects in formerly deficient people and improves their physical state very rapidly. This is not only because of the increased levels of haemoglobin produced but is possibly linked to a number of actions that iron has in the body, which we do not yet understand completely. Further research is needed into the links between iron deficiency, iron supplementation and infectious diseases to discover the additional properties of iron in the body. There are unusual conditions where excessive amounts of iron can accumulate in the tissues. Haemochromatosis, also called bronze diabetes, occurs because of excessive absorption and storage of iron in the liver, spleen and endocrine glands. Liver failure commonly occurs, as does diabetes mellitus and the development of bronze-pigmented skin. Haemosiderosis is a similar condition in which excessive deposition of iron in the body causes damage to various organs, particularly the liver and the heart. The iron is deposited as haemosiderin, a natural iron storage compound. Polycythaemia occurs because of an increase in the number of red blood cells in the blood. Increased levels of platelets and white blood cells are also seen. This condition occurs naturally at high altitudes as a reaction to the lower oxygen content of air but may also be triggered by heart and lung diseases. The cause of the disease is unknown, and treatment is either by removing some blood cells by blood-letting or using cytotoxic drugs to kill some blood cells. A side effect of very high levels of iron in the body is an increased level of receptivity to infectious diseases.

An iron tablet supplement is normally required for pregnant women and anaemic people. Such problems can cause side effects, including stomach pains, diarrhoea, indisposition and constipation. These problems can be reduced if iron is taken after meals, although this has to be balanced against reduced absorption of the mineral. The dose given may have to be reduced if stomach problems arise. In iron-deficient anaemia, it can take up to six months to correct the iron balance in the body. This can be delayed or even impossible if there is internal bleeding because of a stomach ulcer or if there is severe menstrual bleeding. Once the anaemia is corrected, the supplements should be stopped to reduce the risk of excessive iron reserves in the tissues developing. It is best if two hours pass after taking iron supplements before taking other minerals. This is because iron competes with calcium and manganese in the diet, and these minerals can affect the absorption of iron. The other side of the coin is that long-term iron supplements can lead to insufficient levels of calcium and manganese in the body. Some medicines, such as broad-spectrum antibiotics, should not be taken with iron as the drug forms insoluble compounds with mineral salts.

manganese

chemical symbol: Mn

This metal with antioxidant properties is an essential mineral in our bodies. Manganese is found in nuts, tea, whole-grain cereals, vegetables, pulses and avocados. The RDA is 2.5–3.8mg, and most daily intakes are between 5 and 6mg so there is little occurrence of deficiency. Absorption of the mineral is poor, and only 3 per cent of the manganese in food is absorbed in the organism. Manganese is lost through the urine, and this is increased with alcohol intake. The mineral is stored in the cells, primarily in pigmented cells of the skin, hair and the retina of the eye. The role of manganese in the body is for the formation of strong, healthy bones, for healthy nerves and muscles, and for the control of growth. Manganese forms part of the superoxide dismutase (SOD) enzyme system, and it also helps various enzymes to function effectively. The mineral is important for fertility and in the metabolism of carbohydrates and fats. An inadequate supply of manganese results in a decreased growth rate and bone deformities, but such conditions are uncommon. Deficiencies of manganese produced experimentally have symptoms of reduced hair growth, rashes and other skin changes, and emaciation. Insufficient manganese has been proposed as a contributory factor in epilepsy and diabetes, but further work and studies are required to confirm this hypothesis.

Excess intake of manganese can cause brain damage and symptoms similar to those seen in Parkinson's disease. This has been seen in some miners, who would have inhaled manganese oxide while working in unventilated mine shafts. Conventional medicine does not recognize manganese as a therapy, but some nutritional doctors and alternative medicine practitioners use supplements of the mineral to help patients with painful joints and bones. Since manganese activates the body's killer cells, it may be prescribed in cases of cancer. Supplementation should only occur after blood tests are done to check the levels of mineral in the blood. Care should be taken, as manganese competes with iron so absorption of manganese rises if iron is lacking.

molybdenum

chemical symbol: Mo

This is a metallic element whose role in the human body is largely unknown. It is termed an essential trace element as it forms part of at least three enzymes. Molybdenum is found in buckwheat, barley, oats, liver, leguminous fruits and pulses. The content of molybdenum in foodstuffs varies considerably, depending on the level of the mineral found naturally in the soil. Some areas of Russia have high levels of molybdenum in the soil, and this results in a daily intake of 10–15mg, which is almost one hundred times the normal daily intake. The RDA for this mineral ranges from 100 to 500μg, depending on each country's conditions. Molybdenum is taken into the body and distributed throughout the body tissues, and is found in particularly high levels in the liver. Excess molybdenum is excreted in both the urine and the faeces.

There is little known about what molybdenum does in the body, but it is part of at least three active metabolic enzymes that act to neutralize toxic sulphur compounds. Molybdenum is important in the production of haemoglobin, and it is also supposed to help prevent dental caries. This effect has been seen in animals and is backed by evidence that levels of dental decay are lower in molybdenum-rich areas. Molybdenum may also be linked to the male sexual function, although this is as yet unproven. In areas where molybdenum content of the soil, and hence of the diet, is extremely low, high levels of cancer of the oesophagus are seen. This may be caused by a failure of the molybdenum enzyme, leading to an accumulation of carcinogenic nitrogen compounds in the tissues. Some animal studies have backed this idea, but the real story is yet to be confirmed. Levels of molybdenum in the blood serum rise above the normal levels of $1.1 \mu g\ l^{-1}$ during liver diseases. Several hereditary diseases result in poor metabolism of molybdenum as two enzymes, xanthine oxidase and sulphite oxidase, do not function well. Molybdenum supplements do not help prevent the illness, and fortunately these diseases are very rare.

Conflicting evidence is available for the importance of this mineral and for its action on the body. Some sources suggest that inadequate intake of molybdenum may lead to increased levels of dental caries, impotence and, in extreme cases, an irregular heartbeat and coma. These deficiency problems may not be true, and molybdenum needs to be researched thoroughly in order to fill in the gaps in our knowledge of it.

selenium

chemical symbol: Se

Selenium is an element that is essential for human health and is found in the same group of the periodic table as oxygen. Selenium was first discovered in 1817 by Jöns J. Berzelius of Sweden. It is found in unrefined foods, especially whole-grain flour, seafood, egg yolk, fish, cereals and products, liver, kidney, garlic and brewer's yeast. The use of selenium as a therapeutic medicine first started around the 1900s when doctors tried to use selenium to treat cancer in France, Britain, Germany and the United States. Unfortunately, the dosages administered were too high, causing selenium poisoning, and much of the medical profession turned against its medicinal use. Through the 1930s, evidence showing selenium poisoning of animals arose in America. This was because of the high levels of selenium in cattle feed, and experiments have confirmed that large doses of selenium can be toxic for animals. Evidence that selenium may be an important nutrient for humans started to arise in 1941, and in 1949 it was proved that selenium could prevent the formation of liver tumours in rats. The first breakthrough occurred in 1957, when Dr Klaus Schwartz discovered that liver necrosis in rats could be prevented by kidney extract, which contained selenium. Since then, selenium has become the focus of a large programme of research.

Early experiments revealed that selenium could prevent muscular dystrophy in pigs, sheep, hens and calves. It was at this time that selenium was used as an effective remedy for other livestock diseases and that it was first linked to vitamin E. Vitamin E could replace or accompany selenium in treating these livestock diseases. New Zealand was the first country to make widespread use of the mineral to prevent deficiency problems in domestic animals. This occurred in 1967 and was due to the fact that New Zealand is one of the areas in the world with the lowest levels of soil selenium. In the same year, Finnish vets used selenium to treat muscle diseases in domestic animals, and in 1969 veterinary authorities authorized the addition of selenium in animal feeds. Also, since 1984 selenium is added to all artificial fertilizers to increase the selenium intake of agricultural products and hence increase the intake of the human population.

Selenium and health

In the 1970s researchers discovered that selenium could prevent mutations, which are unusual changes in genetic material that may trigger disease. Such mutations may be entirely harmless or they may prevent basic processes required for life, and these changes may be passed on to the next generation. Then, in 1973, the enzyme glutathione peroxidase was found. Glutathione peroxidase contains four atoms of selenium in its structure, and it acts against oxygen-free radicals, hydrogen peroxides and fatty acid peroxides, preventing damage to the cell. This finding proved that selenium was very important in preventing animal diseases. Even today, some health practitioners are sceptical about the importance and benefits that selenium can bring in preventing disease. The first serious cases of selenium deficiency in humans arose in the late 1970s in the province of Keshan in China. People there had developed a disease of the heart, similar to 'mulberry heart' of cattle, in which the heart muscle degenerated with a subsequent loss of power to pump blood around the body. It arose mainly in young women and children in an area with possibly the lowest selenium levels in the world. Without selenium supplementation the disease was fatal. A similar disease affecting the cartilage in the joints, called Kaschin-Beck disease, was found in Russia and China, which again could be prevented and treated with selenium supplements.

Requirements for selenium

The human requirements for selenium are not yet known but an intake of 50–200μg is said to be sufficient. However, a value of 70μg for men and 50μg for women is considered enough to keep the balance of selenium absorbed and excreted in step. This level does not consider the aspect of preventing disease. These levels have been difficult to attain in many areas. Northern Europe has very low selenium levels in the soils and rock. This is because the selenium-rich layers of earth were moved southwards, and the soil left contains little of this micronutrient. This problem has been worsened by the effects of acid rain, pollution and the exhaustion of the soil nutrients, and the excessive use of synthetic fertilizers. As mentioned before, this problem has been partially eradicated by supplementing fertilizers and animal foodstuff with selenium. The lack of the mineral is a particular problem in Scandinavia, where foodstuffs are very low in selenium. The mean daily intake of selenium is 45μg in Denmark and Sweden, 50–70μg in Norway and 90–100μg in Finland, because of the supplements described above. To compare, the Keshan province had a daily intake of less than 10μg per day. This reduced mineral intake shows up in the blood selenium levels. Danes, Swedes, New Zealanders and Egyptians have the lowest recorded levels of selenium in their blood. People in Finland have seen a rise in selenium blood serum from $75\mu gl^{-1}$ to $100\mu gl^{-1}$, but some people still have selenium serum levels below $85\mu gl^{-1}$, which appears to be the critical level below which there is an increased risk of cardiovascular disease and cancer. Whole blood selenium values of between 200 and $350\mu gl^{-1}$ exist because of selenium supplements and confer several protective effects on the body by inhibiting lipid peroxidation and other beneficial effects.

Selenium occurs in an organic form in food, and as both an organic and inorganic form in food supplements. The two types of selenium are absorbed in different ways, with organic selenium being almost totally absorbed (85–95 per cent) but inorganic selenium differing in absorption from 40 to 70 per cent, depending on the type of preparation. Inorganic selenium is lost in the urine when the human body reaches saturation point. Organic selenium is stored in the tissues. In humans there is about $100\mu l^{-1}$, with 60 per cent of that in the red blood cells while 40 per cent is found in the blood serum. The blood moves the mineral round the tissues and there a proportion of the selenium is bound to the glutathione peroxidase enzyme, while the rest of the mineral is bound to haemoglobin and other proteins. Almost half the total 10–15mg of selenium found in the body is stored in the liver. The activity of glutathione peroxidase is correlated to the levels of selenium in the blood until the enzyme activity reaches an optimal level.

Groups at risk of selenium deficiency

Several groups of the population are liable to a reduced intake of selenium. Young people living away from home may not get a balanced diet because of inadequate funds, lack of time for shopping, lack of proper storage facilities or because of a lack of cooking equipment. Studies in Finland have determined that students get less than half of the average daily intake of selenium. This group may also have the lowest blood selenium levels. Vegetarians' intake of selenium may be as low as $10\mu gl^{-1}$ as grains, plants and vegetables are very low in selenium. The elderly may have inadequate selenium intake as they perhaps cannot afford meat or fish, which contain good amounts of the mineral. Other problems may derive from dental problems as elderly people may struggle to chew or eat meat and fish. Smokers have a greater demand for the antioxidant properties of selenium as smoking and drinking alcohol increase the formation of free radicals. Thus smokers require more of the mineral and almost always have lower blood selenium levels than nonsmokers. People suffering from chronic illnesses, including gastrointestinal diseases such as malabsorption or gluten allergy, may be deficient in selenium. Drugs or diseases that cause loss of appetite, diarrhoea, frequent vomiting and unvaried diets can also result in insufficient selenium. Lower blood selenium levels are seen in most cancer patients as well as in heart disease patients. People with arthritis who are treated using cortisone may lack enough selenium. Pregnant women may become deficient in selenium during pregnancy as the foetus takes part of the mother's selenium reserves for use in its body. While breast-feeding, the mother loses selenium as it is passed to her offspring. This loss can not normally be resolved by a change of diet, and selenium supplements are required to keep up with the mineral losses each day.

The action of selenium in the body

Selenium has a number of different tasks in the human body. As mentioned before, selenium is an antioxidant that prevents peroxidation of lipids in the cells. This halts cell damage and slows the pathological ageing process. Glutathione peroxidase breaks down harmful fatty acid peroxide and hydrogen peroxide. This protective action is complemented by vitamin E and helps in the destruction of these free radicals. Enzymes like superoxide dimutase and catalase also take part in the defence system against free radicals.

Selenium boosts the effectiveness of the immune system by improving the operations of the T-lymphocytes and the macrophages, which scavenge the blood for foreign material. The T-lymphocytes are set to recognize bacteria, virus and cancer cells so they can manufacture antibodies against the invading cells faster. A subset of the T-lymphocytes, called killer T-cells, can eliminate cancer cells. The role of the macrophages is to ingest and destroy human cells that have become infected by viruses or bacteria, and this exposed the pathogen to the antibodies and B-cells. It also stops the pathogen replicating further.

Selenium is linked to the prostaglandins, but by which mechanism is yet unknown. There are 'good' and 'bad' prostaglandins, but selenium appears to raise the production levels of the 'good' prostaglandin chemicals (PGE1 and PGE3). These hormone-like unsaturated fatty acids have a substantial regulatory effect on the coagulation of the blood and also influence the occurrence of arteriosclerosis and the clotting of blood platelets. Hence, these substances have a role in preventing thromboses. Low levels of selenium in the blood serum (less than $85 \mu g l^{-1}$) may elevate the chances of having a low level of the HDL-cholesterol, which is the 'good' form, and may increase the risk of a blood clot forming. Low levels of selenium may show as abnormalities on an electrocardiogram and specify heart problems. A low selenium intake seems to be a factor in cases of myocardial infarction and arteriosclerosis.

This mineral has been found to inhibit the toxic effects of heavy metals such as mercury, cadmium, lead and arsenic. The way that selenium protects the body's cells from damage is still to be uncovered. Selenium also protects cells against other harmful substances, like cytotoxic drugs given during chemotherapy. Work has shown that when selenium is given with adriamycin, the adverse side effects are reduced. Adriamycin is a medicine used to treat ovarian cancer, and it encourages the formation of free radicals and is very harmful to the heart and liver. The severity of the action of this drug is tempered by the protective action of selenium.

Selenium and cancer

Experiments on animals have told us that insufficient selenium in our bodies increases the risk of developing cancer. Food supplements of 1–5 parts per million of selenium can repress skin cancer, breast cancer, leukaemia, sarcomas, liver cancer and cancer of the large intestines. Selenium supplements can prevent many cancers forming in animals. This mineral can inhibit the transfer of Bittner's milk virus from the mother to the foetus. This disease occurs in rats, and it and similar viruses are carcinogenic and can be stopped by selenium. These anti-cancer properties can be reinforced by vitamins A and E, when they increase the success rate against cancer in animals from 50 per cent to 90 per cent.

In humans there is a proven link between insufficient selenium and cancer. People with low blood levels of this mineral show a higher occurrence of cancer. This was first detected in the United States in the 1960s because of diet differences from state to state. Many studies have reported that cancer patients with diseases affecting the kidneys, bladder, breast, ovaries, prostate, blood, skin and the rectum show selenium levels in blood and tissue that are 30 per cent lower than those in a healthy control group. One problem with this is that a sick person will not eat the same food or have as good an appetite as a healthy person, so you cannot assume that low selenium status causes cancer. To get over this problem, investigations of healthy people were followed up over many years. These studies showed that the people who developed cancer had low selenium values for years before the disease was detected. Lack of vitamin E and selenium increased the chances of getting cancer by a factor of ten, said one of the recent major studies in Finland. If lack of selenium is associated with deficiencies of other antioxidant vitamins and minerals, e.g. beta-carotene, vitamin A, vitamin E, copper, zinc, manganese, then the probability of getting cancer is heightened further. Selenium appears to fend off cancer in four ways:

1. Selenium protects the cells from damage caused by oxygen-free radicals. These compounds are highly reactive and form peroxides, which accelerate the promotion phase of cancer. This is the stage where precancerous cells are formed.
2. Selenium lowers the mutagenic power of carcinogenic chemicals. This means that the chemicals, viruses and radiation cause less damage to the genetic material in cells.
3. Selenium does not allow carcinogenic viruses to reproduce.
4. Selenium curbs the division of cancer cells and halts them spreading through the tissues.

Despite the myriad activities of selenium, it must not be forgotten that there are many interacting factors that trigger cancers to develop. Selenium has been used since 1911 as a treatment for cancer, boosting antioxidant levels and reinforcing the immune defence. This uses higher doses than are used in preventing disorders, when 200–300μg is the dosage used.

The heart and selenium

Insufficient selenium in cattle causes a disease called 'mulberry heart'. The heart muscle degenerates, and it is left weakened and is unable to pump blood around the body effectively. A similar disease of humans that first arose in the Keshan province in China has been discussed earlier. A few cases of a similar disease appeared, but these were in very ill people who were being drip-fed and who lacked selenium in the parenteral nutrition they were given.

A study carried out in Finland in 1982 showed that when serum levels of selenium were less than $45 \mu g l^{-1}$, the chances of contracting heart disease were elevated by a factor between 2 and 7. This work determined that serum levels of under 85µgl^{-1} were associated with the risk factors leading to coronary heart disease, e.g. increased aggregation of platelets, low HDL-cholesterol, and changes in the electrocardiogram pattern during exercise. People with acute myocardial infarction are frequently lacking in selenium and vitamin B_6. Other antioxidant vitamins such as A, C and E and the mineral zinc can protect the heart from ischaemia and reperfusion injury. Best results are obtained from a mixture of water-soluble and fat-soluble antioxidants. A British investigation done in the late 1980s found that people with heart infarction and arteriosclerosis have quantities of lipid peroxides (rancid fat) in their blood and that this may be the cause of the problem. This theory is backed up by animal experiments. The size of myocardial infarction can be reduced by antioxidants.

Using selenium for chronic diseases

Selenium may be linked with preventing some children's neurological diseases. Therapy with a range of antioxidants has helped children with Becker's muscular dystrophy and Duchennes muscular dystrophy. These are similar diseases that cause chronic muscle degeneration. Becker's occurs between the ages of eight and twenty, while Duchennes appears between the ages of three and five. Duchennes affects the muscles of the legs and pelvis, in particular, producing a waddling gait, inward curvature of the spine and contracture of joints. Fatty deposits may form in the calves and harden the muscle, and antioxidants may help to limit this deposition.

Selenium deficiency may be connected to the lipid peroxidation that occurs in multiple sclerosis. This is a progressive disease in which the nerve fibres lose their protective sheath of myelin, a fatty substance. Myelin allows fast movement of nerve impulses along the fibre, and without the myelin sheath, transfer of nerve impulses to the muscles is vastly impaired or impossible. Loss of myelin may be because of the action of free radicals oxidizing the fatty deposits, and hence antioxidants such as selenium can help stop the loss of myelin.

Since any inflammation response triggers the formation of lipid peroxides and free radicals, selenium and other antioxidants should ease rheumatic pains, stiffness in the joints and arthritic complaints. In some cases, supplementation with selenium has helped in the neurological disease myasthenia gravis. Selenium antioxidants and essential fatty acids can help various allergies, such as asthma, hay fever and eczema. Antioxidants and selenium can benefit injuries to nerves and blood vessels in diabetes, as they are damaged by lipid peroxidation. The use of selenium as a prophylactic drug to prevent diabetic eye conditions has progressed well. Recently, selenium deficiency has been detected in a number of patients suffering from Aids, and supplements of selenium are being tested to see if they have any beneficial impact.

Preparations of selenium

Organic preparations of selenium are best absorbed by the body, but the degree to which the body can use it varies, partly because of differences between the different selenium products on the market. The best combination of antioxidants contains selenium, zinc, and vitamins A, B_6, C and E. This contains selenium in the form of L-selenomethionine, which is a form of organic selenium. Inorganic selenium is not as effective in the body, and to have the same effect as organic selenium a much larger dose is needed.

The effectiveness of organic selenium has been shown in tests of breast-feeding mothers, when it was found that organic selenium is absorbed into the mother's body well and then secreted in the breast milk in good levels. The inorganic selenium had much poorer absorption into the mother's body and was not detected in the breast milk at all. So the method of selenium supplementation and the quality of the products are important to gain maximum benefits in this case.

Selenium is possibly the most important trace mineral in our diet.

It has such a wide range of protective mechanisms and interacts with many other vitamins and minerals. Continuing research will expand our knowledge about the actions and behaviour of selenium in the human body.

silicon

chemical symbol: Si

Silicon is found in the same group of the periodic table as carbon and has similar chemical properties. This mineral has only been recognized as essential for humans recently, and little is known about its uptake, metabolism and function in our bodies. Silicon occurs in nature mainly as silicon dioxide and as silicate salts. Much of the silicon in our diet comes from milk and vegetables. The mineral is absorbed from the intestines and transported in the blood to the muscles, bones, sinews, nails, cartilage and the brain. Quite large amounts of silicon are contained in the lymph glands. Much of the silicon taken into the human body is excreted in the urine. As yet, the level of silicon required by the human body is unknown, and there are no official RDAs. The average human contains around 7g of the mineral, which is more than for iron or copper, and this suggests that the daily requirement is approximately 20–30mg. Whether or not silicon is deficient in our diets is difficult to decide as we do not know what the optimal levels of silicon are, and it is as yet hard to tell how to measure the levels of silicon in the blood. There is no known deficiency disease linked to silicon.

Like selenium, the organic forms of silicon seem to be absorbed and utilized far more effectively by the body than inorganic silicon. Silicon seems to have the ability to stimulate the osteoblast cells, which make bone. It is also important in making the starting material for the connective tissues. Large concentrations of silicon are found in the osteoblasts and are vital in the activity of these cells. The mineral helps to form the proteins collagen and elastin, which allow connective tissues to contract and become elastic. Silicon has become popular in strengthening hair and nail growth, but these beneficial effects have not been backed by controlled studies. Investigations have proved the benefits silicon brings in encouraging bone formation, and supplements of silicon, fluorine and boron have been recommended to aid healing after a fractured bone. People fitted with a replacement hip joint as a result of fracture or osteoarthritis can benefit from supplements of silicon and boron, which will help new bone mass grow around the new joint and hold it in position. This is especially valuable in elderly people, whose bone growth is slower than in young people. There is a possibility that silicon may be good in preventing and treating osteoporosis. Research is needed to determine how calcium, magnesium, silicon and boron work together to allow bone formation.

Silicon may be linked to the development of arteriosclerosis, as the levels of silicon in the artery walls fall with age, and with the start of arteriosclerosis. This lowering of silicon values may cause arteriosclerosis or it may be an effect of the disease. Silicon would appear to help inflammatory reactions as well. The experience of some nutritional doctors shows that supplements of silicon may help strengthen skin, hair and nails and can treat inflammatory skin complaints such as atopic eczema.

zinc

chemical symbol: Zn

Zinc is a metallic element that is very important for good health. It is involved in many processes in the body and controls the functioning of many enzymes. The average human adult contains 2–4g of zinc, of which 78 per cent is held in the bones, muscles and the skin. These tissues store the mineral, and if a deficiency of the mineral arises then the zinc is released. Hence, we require a daily intake of zinc in our diet.

The RDA for zinc is 15mg for adults, but most people do not get this level in their diet. Groups particularly at risk of insufficient zinc are growing children, the elderly, pregnant women, vegetarians and people suffering from chronic illnesses or allergies. During pregnancy and breast-feeding, the levels of zinc required rise by 50 to 75 per cent to 23–27mg daily. Zinc is found in liver, red meat, egg yolk, whole-grain flour, seafood (especially oysters), dairy produce, vegetables, and cereals and their products. The percentage of zinc absorbed in the body is variable, and in a mixed diet of meat and vegetables roughly 15–40 per cent of the zinc intake is absorbed. Zinc in vegetables is not absorbed as well, so vegetarians are at a particular risk of deficiency, and supplementation may be sensible. The best form of zinc, which is absorbed well, is organic zinc, normally as gluconate or aspartate salts. Care should be taken with zinc supplements as zinc competes with copper, and higher levels of zinc intake can reduce the absorption of copper. Any zinc supplement of more than 30mg daily taken to augment the dietary intake should be combined with a small supplement of copper to prevent any problems arising. Zinc is taken in via the intestines and is removed from the body with secretions from the gall bladder and pancreas and with the excreted material. Loss of zinc increases because of diabetes, dialysis treatment, diuretic medicine, some anti-arthritis medicines and excessive sweat production. Tissue damage caused by kidney diseases, flaking skin diseases or burns also cause more zinc to be lost from the body.

Zinc has a multitude of roles in the body. It forms part of the active site of around 200 enzymes, including carbonic anhydrases and dehydrogenases involved in energy metabolism. These enzymes work to form bone tissue, to heal wounds and sores, to produce protein and to regulate the carbohydrate metabolism. Other enzymes are involved in regulating the synthesis of ribosomes and ribonucleic acids. Deficiency of zinc inhibits the growth of children. The mineral forms an essential part of the CuZn superoxide dismutase (SOD) enzyme, which is an antioxidant that neutralizes harmful free radicals. Zinc helps boost the immune system against invading viruses, bacteria, allergens and carcinogens, and inadequate zinc intake lessens our disease resistance. Other of the enzymes activated by zinc is the enzyme that converts retinol to retinal, which is used to form eye pigments. Lack of zinc means the body cannot utilize the vitamin A it receives in the diet and the body is lacking in the antioxidant vitamin A. Zinc also forms part of the enzyme that allows the release of insulin from the pancreas. Zinc is also needed to transform one of the essential fatty acids, linoleic acid, into gamma-linolenic acid, which is required for the production of 'good' prostaglandins.

Zinc deficiency causes problems with the skin, because 20 per cent of the body's reserves are stored in the skin, and this tissue reacts fast to deficiency conditions. Insufficient zinc can also cause slow physical, mental and sexual development. It can affect and reduce the healing of wounds, and it may be important in infertility. Inadequate zinc levels can cause decreased alertness, poor appetite, increased susceptibility to infection and injury, retarded growth and a loss of the sense of smell. Hormonal disturbances, general fatigue and losing the sense of taste can result from too little zinc. This mineral has attracted a great deal of attention lately as lack of zinc appears to be connected with dysfunctions of the brain, such as dyslexia. In a British study, children with the condition had zinc values a third lower than their classmates without the condition. This was followed up by an investigation in Finland, where 18 children with dyslexia were given supplements of 15mg of zinc and 100µg of selenium daily. Analysis showed that prior to the study 13 out of the 18 children had lower zinc concentrations in their blood than normal. After eight months of supplementation, 11 children showed significant improvements and had less difficulty in reading and writing. The schoolteachers reported a substantial improvement was seen in the whole class after only two months of mineral supplementation. Many in the medical profession believe that dyslexia may derive from zinc deficiencies in one of the parents when the child is conceived. Zinc is also thought to be linked with the circumference of the baby's skull. Low zinc levels in the placenta are associated with small skull circumference and related delays in brain development.

Zinc is used as a therapy for several diseases, including acne, heart diseases, stomach ulcers and arthritis, and benefits the healing of skin wounds as it speeds up the healing process. The mineral may be good used before and after operations to aid healing. When taken in combination with vitamins A, B_6, C and E, zinc is very helpful for skin diseases and allergic problems like hay fever. Zinc should be taken by cancer patients as it helps to limit the spread of the tumour, and a dose of 15–30mg per day would be most effective. The mineral is being used to treat an eye disease, called senile degeneration of the macula, which causes impaired sight or blindness in elderly people. The disease is caused or worsened by free radicals, and the zinc forms part of essential enzymes that are needed for correct eye functioning.

Fortunately, zinc is not too toxic, and side effects are unlikely even with considerable overdosing. In doses of more than 30mg per day, when taken for a period of time, it is best to take a copper supplement, both to avoid copper deficiency and to avoid a possible increase in the cholesterol levels in the blood.

Trace Elements

arsenic

chemical symbol: As

Many people will wonder about including this mineral in a list of minerals essential for health. Arsenic has been seen as a poison for many years, and recent medical studies have shown that arsenic may be required, in small quantities, for the correct functioning of the human body. An adult contains about 14mg of arsenic, and it is estimated that the daily requirements are between 0.5 and 4.0mg. Arsenic is stored in all the tissues, especially the hair and nails. Investigations using experimental animals showed that when the dietary intake of arsenic is less than 0.5mg per kilogram of body weight, the animals' growth and fertility are affected and their internal organs are at risk from damage. Arsenic is used in some drugs to try and kill the *Trypanosomas* parasite, which is found in Africa and Central and South America and which is transmitted to humans by various insects. Poisoning by arsenic can be chronic, with symptoms of nausea, headache, dry and pigmented skin, hair loss and tiredness, or acute, which shows as nausea, diarrhoea, vomiting and sweating, all stemming from inflammation of the stomach lining. Poisoning by arsenic can be counteracted by selenium, and vice versa. Environmental exposure to arsenic, e.g. through mining, can give rise to a specific form of lung cancer. The incidence of this cancer is reduced if the miners have high levels of selenium in their blood.

boron

chemical symbol: B

The element is similar to aluminium, and it is the subject of a lot of medical and scientific studies that show it is an essential trace element. Boron is essential to animals and plants. It is found in tomatoes, pears, prunes, raisins, dates, berries, apples, citrus fruits and avocados. Wine, soya meal, nuts, and honey are also rich in boron. At the moment, there is no RDA for boron, but it has been calculated that 1–2mg of boron per day may meet the human requirement. Most people consume between 1 and 2mg of boron each day, although intakes of only 0.25mg have been seen. The levels of boron in fruit and vegetables depends on the levels of the mineral in the soil. Mauritius and Jamaica have low levels of boron and may not get enough boron in their diet. The levels of the mineral in the blood and tissues are sensitive to the variations in diet from day to day, and vegetarians may benefit from the higher levels of boron in their diets from the vegetables.

The main role of boron in the body is unknown, but it appears to be important in preventing and treating osteoporosis and rheumatoid arthritis. People with rheumatoid arthritis or similar joint diseases have significantly lower levels of boron in their bones, when compared to healthy people. Workers in New Zealand found that a daily supplement of 6–9mg of boron would reverse the symptoms in 80–90 per cent of patients within a few weeks of treatment. Boron was also found to cure arthritis in cattle, dogs and horses. Boron in the form of borax ($Na_2B_4O_7.IOH_2O$) has been used to help arthritis in New Zealand and Australia. Countries like Israel, which has high levels of boron in the soil, have virtually no incidence of arthritis, while Jamaica and Mauritius have low soil boron levels and a high incidence of arthritis.

Studies completed by the United States Department of Agriculture show that a supplement of 3mg of boron reduces the amounts of magnesium, calcium and phosphorus excreted in the urine of post-menopausal women. An additional benefit of this therapy was that oestrogen levels in the blood were increased by 100 per cent after only eight days of treatment. This is of great importance as oestrogen reduces demineralization of bones after the menopause.

All this evidence points to the idea that dietary deficiency of boron may be involved in osteoporosis in women after the menopause. It would seem that a supplement of 3mg of boron each day would help both prevent and treat osteoporosis and rheumatoid arthritis. Boron may benefit people with allergic reactions as people who suffer from allergic rashes generally have low levels of boron present in their skin.

lead

chemical symbol: Pb

Lead is a metallic element that some sources believe is required by the body in very small quantities. Lead salts may be applied to wounds, when it helps to stop bleeding, reduces inflammation and provides a protective covering over the wound. Large doses of soluble lead salts irritate the stomach. Lead is well known as a poison, and this chronic poisoning occurs most often because of exposure in the workplace. Plumbers, pottery workers, dyers, lead smelters and people cleaning petrol storage tanks are most at risk. Lead may be derived from drinking water contaminated with lead, and the risks are particularly high in areas with soft or peaty water, which are more capable of dissolving lead. Lead can be inhaled as dry dust, absorbed through the skin, or absorbed via the stomach from the diet and water supply. Symptoms of chronic poisoning can start with muscular weakness, constipation, pale skin and colic. The formation of a blue line marking the gums is characteristic of lead poisoning along with anaemia, anorexia and damage to the nervous system causing muscle tremors and paralysis. Lead also causes damage to the kidney function, blindness (temporary or permanent) because of nerve damage, convulsions and death if treatment cannot halt the damage and exposure continues. Acute poisoning is similar, causing abdominal pains, diarrhoea, vomiting and possibly developing into convulsions and paralysis. Treatment is with a chelating agent, which removes the lead from the circulation, and it is eliminated from the body. Evidence varies as to whether lead is important in human health, but its deleterious effects are common knowledge.

nickel

chemical symbol: Ni

This element is a metal, and it is essential for the human body's requirements. Nickel is found in vegetables, explaining why vegetarians tend to have a higher intake of it than people with a mixed meat and vegetable diet. There is no RDA established for nickel, but daily intakes vary from 130 to 400μg. It is poorly absorbed in the intestines, with only 10 per cent absorbed, and this does not increase as intake increases. The excess nickel is eliminated from the body in the faeces, with smaller amounts lost through sweating and in the urine. The normal serum blood levels of nickel are around 1.5–5.0μgl^{-1}. Much of the evidence for nickel being an essential trace element comes from animal experiments, where nickel deficiency leads to a range of complaints. Rats and pigs have reduced growth and lowered fertility when nickel is lacking, and hens show changes to the blood, liver and skin. There are no recognized deficiency diseases for nickel in humans, but it has been discovered that levels in the blood increase when the heart is lacking in oxygen (ischaemia). The nickel in the blood is not released from the heart muscle, and this change is not yet fully understood. It does allow examination of blood nickel values to identify ischaemic heart disease and to determine the level of damage after a heart attack.

Recent studies from Denmark have shown that high blood levels of nickel may be linked to arthritis. Nickel is contained in drinking water as it is released from the metal pipes. This can be a particular occurrence in water that has been left standing in pipes all night, and it can be exceedingly high in the mineral. It is advisable to let water run for a time to reduce the level of nickel in it. Nickel in the diet can cause allergic eczema and in wristwatches or jewellery it can cause an allergic contact dermatitis. Some people even have an allergic reaction to the nickel in coins.

There are no health reasons for using nickel to prevent or treat illness, and nickel carbonyl compounds used in industry are known to be carcinogenic.

tin

chemical symbol: Sn

This is a metal that is vital for proper functioning of the human body. In animal experiments, it was found that rats need 1–2mg of tin per kilogram of body weight so normal growth and development can occur. The level of requirement by humans has not been determined, and there is no RDA set. Fresh food normally contains 1mg of tin in every kilogram of food, while the level of tin in tinned or deep-frozen food is generally 2mg per kilogram of foodstuff. Thus the tin intake varies depending on the amount of frozen or tinned food consumed, from 0.2 to 17mg per day. In the United States, 15 per cent of total food eaten is from tins so they probably have the largest consumption of the mineral. Like selenium and chromium, inorganic salts of tin are absorbed to a much lower extent than organic tin. Both types of tin are excreted differently, with organic tin being lost along with the faeces and inorganic tin with the urine.

The main role of tin is to contribute to the absorption of several other minerals and trace elements. It inhibits the absorption of zinc and copper into some tissues and limits their elimination from the body. In some cases, it can increase the removal of zinc with the urine. Tin does not appear to affect the excretion of manganese, iron or magnesium. Tin does play an important role in the metabolism of bone tissue, possibly in conjunction with vitamin D. Experiments with animals have shown that tin has differing effects on the immune system. Some strengthen the immune system and others may weaken it. It is possible that the growth of cancerous tissue may be halted to some degree by supplementation of the diet with tin. This response may occur through the action of the immune system or the mineral may act on the cells directly. Tin is only slightly toxic, but there is too little evidence to back the use of tin as a treatment for disease. The actions of tin on the immune system and on cancer may become more valuable in the future.

tungsten

chemical symbol: W

This metal normally occurs in nature in compounds of iron. Tungsten is a component of most mixed diets, but it has not been determined whether or not this mineral is an essential trace element. There is currently little information about average daily intakes, and no RDA is established. Tungsten from the diet is stored in the liver, bones and kidneys.

Tungsten has a mutual relationship with other trace elements, especially copper and molybdenum. Absorption of molybdenum from the intestines can be obstructed by tungsten, and it modifies the activity of the enzyme xanthine oxidase, which requires molybdenum to function effectively.

Tungsten itself is not too toxic, but some forms, e.g. tungsten carbide, are liable to cause lung damage. There are no current uses for tungsten in either preventing or treating disease.

vanadium

chemical symbol: V

This metal is recognized as an essential trace element, but unfortunately relatively little is known about it. Vanadium is found in some plants and vegetables, particularly radishes and dill, and only 1 per cent of this mineral from our diet is absorbed into the body, with the rest being removed via the urine. There are no set requirements for vanadium, but we are estimated to need between 1 and 4mg daily. The amount of vanadium present in the average diet is also unknown. The vanadium that is taken into the body is metabolized by a route that we do not know, but most tissues contain vanadium but in quantities that have not yet been worked out. Blood serum levels of vanadium are less than $10\mu g l^{-1}$.

Most of the information about vanadium relates to work completed on animals. Research in 1971 found that rats that had been lacking in vanadium for a long period of time gained approximately 40 per cent of their body weight when they were fed vanadium supplements of sodium orthovanadate. Deficiency in vanadium led to retarded development of chickens and, unexpectedly, to lowered cholesterol levels. These observations cannot be directly transferred to humans. Studies have shown that vanadium can curb the development of spontaneous tumours in animals and may lessen the carcinogenic properties of some chemicals. Conflicting reports on the action of vanadium salts are known, and some studies show that these salts can destroy cancer cells. It is to be hoped that our knowledge about this element and its importance in humans will increase in the future.

Other Minerals

aluminium

chemical symbol: Al

There is considerable debate as to whether aluminium has any benefits to human health. The human requirements for the mineral are not known, but the amount of aluminium in the diet varies from 7mg in Finland, 80mg in Norway to 100mg in the United States. The higher two values take into account aluminium that enters food from the surface of aluminium cooking pots, other kitchen utensils and disposable juice cartons coated with aluminium. It also enters our bodies from environmental pollution in the air, and these unusual sources of the mineral can be quite significant. Aluminium is the third most abundant element in the earth's crust, making up 8 per cent of it. Aluminium is released from the soil by the action of acid rain lowering the pH, and the mineral then enters the ground water and may be taken into supplies of drinking water. Concentrations of aluminium in drinking water in Norway and the United Kingdom seem to correlate to the prevalence of Alzheimer's disease. This possibility is currently being researched further, and more information as to the mechanism of the link is awaited, but it has been proposed that the disease results from the deposition of aluminium in the brain cells, which would impair their functioning.

Aluminium forms part of our diet as instant coffee, table salt, dried milk, some food additives and in tea bags. The mineral is also a component of many stomach medicines, including anti-acid tablets, that can increase the levels of aluminium excreted in the urine by 800 per cent and the excretion of zinc by 125 per cent. Aluminium hydroxide in stomach medicines also binds to phosphates and means they cannot be taken up by the body. This can lead to inadequate levels of phosphorus in the body. Several vaccines for diseases also contain aluminium.

Aluminium is an extremely reactive chemical, and it is inclined to bind to other substances. Since aluminium ions (Al^{3+}) are similar to iron (Fe^{3+}), aluminium can change places with iron in proteins such as ferritin (*see* iron in Microminerals) and so enter the cells. When in the body, aluminium causes demineralization of the bones, changes the metabolism of calcium and allows cross-linkages to form in collagen. The mineral also brings about zinc loss, and this may play a part in the development of dementia. Dyslexic people often have high levels of aluminium and low levels of zinc in the body. When zinc is lacking, aluminium can bind to proteins that carry zinc, and supplementation with zinc is necessary to reverse the deficiency, correct the protein structures and restore normal function to many enzyme complexes.

Patients who are drip-fed or who need dialysis treatment absorb much more aluminium than normal people, and this can cause damage to bones and brain damage. This is why dialysis fluids are normally purified and the aluminium removed because aluminium poisoning can be fatal.

silver

chemical symbol: Ag

This element is not required by the human body for any metabolic processes. It is used in medicine as an antiseptic and astringent, and has been used against warts and to stop nosebleeds. In studies of experimental animals, silver given in the diet was only slightly absorbed into the body (10 per cent of the total). The mineral is transported to the liver and stored there. It is not known if the same process happens in humans.

Silver has mutual effects with the minerals copper and selenium and with vitamin E. This means that silver can protect an organism against overdoses and poisoning by these substances, and vice versa. Chronic silver poisoning shows as a permanent blue colouring of the connective membrane in the eye. Poisoning by silver salts, such as silver nitrate, causes discolouring of the lips, abdominal pains, dizziness, vomiting and convulsions.

gold

chemical symbol: Au

Gold is similar to silver in that it is not an essential mineral for humans. It is used to treat some diseases. Gold was first used as a medicine by Jacques Forestier, a Frenchman, about in the middle of the 20th century. He thought that rheumatoid arthritis might be a form of tuberculosis and, as such a serious illness, it would have to be treated with the most expensive medicines. Gold salts are absorbed from the gastrointestinal tract very poorly and have mainly been replaced by chelate gold preparations, which enter the blood and tissues easily. This mineral has also been administered as intramuscular injections, and this produces high concentrations of gold in the tissues. Approximately 5 per cent of the gold administered is excreted after a day, and 85 per cent of the dose is still present after one week. Gold is still being eliminated with the urine as long as one year after injection.

The main use of gold is as treatment for rheumatoid arthritis, as it appears to subdue the inflammatory response in the joints. How this occurs is not entirely understood, but a Japanese study proposed that gold functioned as an antioxidant. This belief may be correct as supplementation with the antioxidants selenium and zinc does not conflict with the use of gold as a therapy. Metallic gold is used by dentists for filling teeth, but has also been utilized in surgery and to treat asthma and skin diseases. Gold is not an essential mineral so it can cause side effects in some patients, with itching, serious kidney damage and rashes. The level of kidney damage is not linked to the dose given but to the degree of sensitivity of the patient to gold treatment. Unfortunately, gold can cause serious toxicity in 10 per cent of patients treated for rheumatoid arthritis and has some toxic reaction in between 25 per cent and 50 per cent of them.

Essential Fatty Acids

Essential fatty acids (EFA) were previously called the F vitamins. They are a group of polyunsaturated fatty acids that are vital for the proper functioning, growth and maintenance of the body. Our requirements of these substances are met entirely through our diet, and deficiencies can occur in some circumstances. We are recommended that at least 10–15 per cent of our intake of calories should come from essential fatty acids. The first EFA was discovered in 1929, and we now know of 12 essential fatty acids, but only linoleic and linolenic acids are required in the diet as the body can transform them into all the other EFAs.

The main essential fatty acids are:

—linoleic acid: found in seed oils of blackcurrants, sunflowers, maize, peanuts, borage and evening primrose.

—gamma-linolenic acid (GLA): found in the seeds of borage, evening primrose and blackcurrants and also in breast milk.

—dihomo-gamma-linolenic acid (DHGLA): contained in offal and breast milk.

—alpha-linolenic acid: found in linseed, soya beans and vegetables.

—arachidonic acid: contained in dairy products, meat, marine algae and prawns.

—eicosapentaenoic acid (EPA): found in marine algae, fish liver oil and fatty fish, e.g. salmon, herring, mackerel.

—docosahexanoic acid (DHA): found in fish, fish liver oil and marine algae.

Interest in these chemicals has increased in recent years, and there are many medical studies being carried out to determine if they can prevent or treat diseases successfully. Most of this work is centred on the effect of EFAs on heart disease, failure of the immune system, disorders of the central nervous system, and allergies. The EFAs are important as the cell membranes are all made up of fatty acids, and these membranes are critical for cell functioning so a lack of EFAs can give rise to serious tissue problems. EFAs are also required as precursors of prostaglandins (PG) and leukotrienes, which are hormone-like substances. Leukotrienes are made from arachdonic acid and are important in inflammation and allergic reactions. They can cause swelling and fluid accumulation in tissues and cause a very strong contraction of the respiratory passages (around 1000 times stronger contraction than is caused by histamine). Prostaglandins have a larger role and work in the human body to regulate calcium metabolism, control the activity of key enzymes and regulate the content of some nucleotides, which have a high energy content. They have a large effect on smooth muscle, particularly in contracting or relaxing the uterus, and they can dilate or constrict blood vessels and so control blood flow. This process has been shown to help the secretion of hormones by increasing the blood flow through endocrine glands. Prostaglandins are also released during an inflammatory response. Some prostaglandins are beneficial to health (PGE1 and PGE3) while others can be harmful (PGE2). PGE1 works to discourage the aggregation of blood platelets and so obstruct formation of blood clots. It can permit expansion of blood vessels and helps to prevent infection of the body by viruses or bacteria. Various prostaglandins are associated with regulating the activity of T-lymphocytes in the immune system.

Arachidonic acid also gives rise to prostaglandins as well as the leukotrienes. Prostacyclin (PGE2) acts in a similar manner to PGE1 and expands blood vessels and helps to prevent blood clots. The only other harmful essential fatty acid is thromboxane A2(TXA2), which contracts the blood vessels, causes inflamed tissues to deteriorate and causes blood clotting.

So in order to prevent or treat any diseases, we must be able to regulate the metabolism of essential fatty acids, leukotrienes and prostaglandins. We can do this by using vitamins, minerals and EFAs instead of anti-inflammatory medicines, steroids and aspirin-based drugs. Vitamin E is known to inhibit the formation of harmful prostaglandins, and selenium, zinc, vitamins B and C are all required to produce beneficial prostaglandins.

gamma-linolenic acid (GLA)
chemical formula: $C_{17}H_{29}COOH$
This is the most important essential fatty acid in our diets. The linoleic acid that we take in via our diet is biologically inactive and has to be converted into GLA. This occurs because of the action of the enzyme delta-6-desaturase (d6d), which requires zinc to function properly. Unfortunately, the action of this enzyme can be stopped by some foodstuffs, medicines, diseases and stimulants, and so linoleic acid is not converted to GLA.

Most people will be lacking in GLA at some point as even a diet rich in plant oils does not stop deficiencies of GLA occurring. The transformation of linoleic acid to GLA is so easily disrupted that it seems that most people would benefit from a supplement of GLA. The most important of these disruptive factors are: a high content of saturated fats in the diet; cholesterol; polyunsaturated fats; diabetes; alcohol; viral infection; cancer; radiotherapy and chemotherapy; vitamin and mineral deficiencies, especially of zinc, magnesium and vitamin B_6; smoking; ageing.

A collection of medicines stops the conversion of linoleic acid, including aspirin-based drugs, cortisone, beta-blockers and anti-arthritis medicines. An unbalanced diet with too much sugar and protein intake reduces the activity of GLA in the body.

So with all these things against an adequate supply of GLA, it should be taken as a food supplement. GLA is obtained from various plant sources that are rich in GLA. The best of these is borage (*Borago officinalis*), which contains 25 per cent of GLA, then blackcurrant seed oil with 14 per cent, and the most common, evening primrose oil, which has 7–9 per cent GLA. To obtain the benefits of GLA, other substances such as vitamin B_6, zinc and selenium need to be present at adequate levels in the diet. When all these substances are present, the body produces more PGE1, one of the 'good' prostaglandins. It acts to reduce the risk of blood clots by inhibiting the blood platelets from sticking together, and it expands blood vessels, particularly when contracted in an attack of angina pectoris. By doing this, it eases the pain of an angina attack.

PGE1 also expands the respiratory airways and prevents mucous forming and asthma attacks. This discourages the onset of lung infections. The prostaglandin reduces the production of cholesterol, boosts the effects of insulin and enhances the activity of the immune system by acting on the T-lymphocytes. This boosted immune system can help rectify problems caused by an upset in immune function, such as allergies, asthma, skin diseases, ulcerative colitis, and arthritis and similar complaints. GLA can be given as a therapy for hangovers and excessive consumption of alcohol, liver damage because of alcohol, hyperactivity in children, and chest pains, aching limbs and oedema. This essential fatty acid can be of considerable benefit to women suffering from premenstrual tension and menstrual pains caused by the increased activity of 'bad' prostaglandins. Levels of GLA and PGE1 appear to be abnormally low in people suffering from disorders of the central nervous system, such as schizophrenia and sclerosis. Some of the studies currently under way would seem to indicate that huge doses of GLA may be able to help treat some cancers.

There are some nutritional doctors who have used GLA in treating asthma, arthritis and atopic eczema with good results. GLA may be given in conjunction with fish oils containing eicosapentanoic acid (EPA) and docosahexanoic acid (DHA) to balance both types of essential fatty acid. Successful results are not always guaranteed in cases of arthritis, as some people take cortisone or other anti-inflammatory drugs, which oppose the benefits of GLA. Better preparations of GLA are arriving on the market all the time, with a greatly increased content of GLA per capsule, which reduces both the cost and the number of capsules needed to be taken each day. The initial high dosage required to treat some complaints does not need to be sustained, and the dose can be reduced to the minimum dose and the treatment is still effective. When taking any supplement of essential fatty acids, the body should have sufficient antioxidants to stop the possible rancification of the EFAs.

eicosapentanoic acid (EPA) *and* **docosahexanoic acid (DHA)** These essential fatty acids are also known as omega–3 fatty acids or fish oils. Their reputation as beneficial for health has hugely increased in recent years, and several studies have confirmed their worth. The human body can produce EPA and DHA from linoleic acid but not in adequate quantities. In the diet they are found in fish, especially fatty fish like salmon, herring and mackerel, fish oils, marine algae, linseeds, and in meat from marine mammals, such as seals and whales, which are eaten in certain cultures. Interest arose when it was found that Eskimos and Japanese fishermen, both groups who ate a lot of fish, had a very low occurrence of heart disease. This connection was then studied in large controlled tests, and a significant link does occur between high intake of fish (and so EPA and DHA) and vastly reduced levels of heart disease. These studies also showed that the incidence of psoriasis, diabetes, asthma and sclerosis were rarer in the groups with a fish-rich diet.

Heart disease is connected to the amount of food consumed and the way in which our diet is balanced between protein, carbohydrate and fats. Generally, the more fat in the diet the higher the risk of heart disease. The levels of cholesterol in the blood as LDL-cholesterol (and its oxidized form o-LDL) increase the risk of hardening of the coronary arteries, while HDL-cholesterol is the protective form of the substance. The impact of cholesterol levels can build up over the long term, even over decades, against the action of dietary fat levels, which affect the aggregation of blood platelets and blood clot formation directly. The tendency of platelets to gather is increased by saturated fats in the diet, and polyunsaturated fats, especially fish oils, discourage this aggregation.

The actions of EPA and DHA are linked to the production of prostaglandins and leukotrienes. These hormone-like substances act in a localized way in the body and are described in the section on gamma-linolenic acid (GLA) above. Fish oils shift the balance towards prostaglandins, which reduce the risks of blood clot formation. EPA and DHA are transformed into prostaglandins, such as thromboxane A3(TXA3) and prostacyclin (PGE13), which lower the aggregation of platelets in the blood. EPA and DHA also allow the blood cells to pass through the blood capillaries. These capillaries are the smallest blood vessels in the body and are only wide enough to allow red blood cells through in a single stream, approximately 7–10µm in diameter. This is why EPA and DHA can help prevent ischaemic heart disease, as they prevent blood cells sticking in the tiny vessels and causing oxygen deficiency in the heart tissue.

Fish oils have been shown to help chronic conditions such as psoriasis, migraines, arthritis and atopic eczema. This is why most governments and health authorities encourage people to eat fish at least twice a week. Along with that, they advise a reduction in the intake of animal fats, which directly oppose the beneficial effects of fish oils. There are now many products containing fish oil, of varying quality. Capsules of fish oil cannot give rise to the allergic reactions some people have to the protein contained in fish flesh. Fish oils, which contain free fatty acids, have an excellent rate of uptake into the body and would be the most effective preparation currently available.

As with GLA, the polyunsaturated fatty acids EPA and DHA in the diet and supplements are very easily oxidized in the body, so care should be taken to ensure an adequate intake of antioxidants such as selenium and vitamin E so that the benefits to health are not lost.

Appendix

RDA values (recommended dietary allowance)

Vitamin or mineral	*RDA range*
A	4–5000 IU retinol; 750–1000μg; 4.5mg beta-carotene
B_1	1.0–1.5mg
B_2	1.1–3.0mg
B_3	18–20mg niacin; 1.08mg tryptophan
B_5	5–50mg
B_6	1.5–2.2mg
B_9	200–400μg
B_{12}	1–6μg
C	30mg/60mg
D	400 IU; 2.5–10μg
E	12–30 IU; 10mg
K	either 70–140μg (0.07–0.14mg) or > 1mg
biotin	0.1mg–0.3mg
calcium	500–1000mg
chlorine	no RDA
chromium	50–200μg
cobalt	no RDA
copper	50–2500μg
fluorine	1–4mg
iodine	100–200μg
iron	10–18mg
magnesium	300–450mg
manganese	2.5–3.8mg

molybdenum	100–500µg
phosphorus	800–1000mg
potassium	1–6g
selenium	50–200µg
sodium	2–3g
zinc	15mg
arsenic	0.5–4.0mg safe intake
boron	1–2mg safe intake
bromine	1.5–2.5mg normal dietary intake
nickel	130–400µg normal dietary intake
tin	0.2–17mg normal dietary intake
vanadium	1–4mg estimated dietary requirement
aluminium	7–100mg normal dietary intake
tungsten	no RDA

Glossary of Medical Terms

acetylcholine an important organic chemical substance present in the body, which is known as a neurotransmitter and is involved in the transmission of electrical impulses along nerves.

acne a disorder of the skin, the commonest of which is *Acne vulgaris* in adolescents, characterized by the presence of pustules and blackheads. Sebaceous glands in the skin become overactive (because of hormonal influence), and there is a greater production of sebum and proliferation of bacteria, which cause infection. The hair follicles become blocked, and pustules form, which eventually turn black. The condition usually resolves with time but can be eased with creams and sometimes antibiotics.

acute a disease or condition that is short-lived and that starts rapidly with severe symptoms.

adenosine triphosphate (ATP) a nucleotide made up of deoxyribose sugar and adenine, to which three phosphate groups are attached. It is essential for life as a carrier of chemical energy in all living organisms. ATP is generated from adenosine diphosphate (ADP) by photosynthesis in plants and during glycolysis, the Krebs cycle and oxidative phosphorylation in animals and humans.

adjuvant therapy a type of drug therapy used in the management of certain cancers following on from radiotherapy or surgical removal of a primary tumour. The aim is to destroy secondary tumours where there is a risk of these occurring, and it is sometimes used in the treatment of breast cancer.

allergy a state of hypersensitivity in an affected individual to a particular allergen, which produces a characteristic response whenever the person is exposed to the substance. In an unaffected person, antibodies present in the bloodstream destroy their particular antigens (allergens). However, in an affected individual this reaction causes some cell damage, and there is a release of substances such as histamine and bradykin, which cause the allergic reaction. Examples of allergies are dermatitis, hay fever, asthma and the severe response known as anaphylaxis.

alternative medicine the name for all forms of healing other than western-orientated medical practice. It includes herbal remedies, acupuncture, homoeopathy, osteopathy, naturopathy and faith healing.

Alzheimer's disease the commonest cause of dementia afflicting those in middle or old age, and a degenerative disease of the cerebral cortex for which there is no cure. Symptoms include progressive loss of memory and speech and paralysis.

amino acids the end products of the digestion of protein foods and the building blocks from which all the protein components of the body are built up. They all contain an acidic carboxyl group (-COOH) and an amino group (-NH_2), which are both bonded to the same central carbon atom. Some can be manufactured within the body whereas others, the essential amino acids, must be derived from protein sources in the diet.

anaemia a decrease in the ability of the blood to carry oxygen because of a reduction in the number of red blood cells or in the amount of haemoglobin that they contain. Haemoglobin is the pigment within the red blood cells that binds to oxygen. There are a number of different types of anaemia and a variety of reasons for it, and treatment depends upon the underlying cause.

analogue a substance that is different in molecular structure from its parent compound but has different effects. An analogue of vitamin E is water-soluble compared to its fat-soluble parent vitamin. Analogues can be more effective and have fewer side effects than other related drugs or substances.

angina a suffocating, choking pain, usually used in reference to angina pectoris, that is felt in the chest. The pain is felt or brought on by exercise and relieved by rest, and occurs when the blood supply to the heart muscle is inadequate. During exercise the demand for blood (supplied by the coronary arteries) is increased, and if the supply is insufficient, because the arteries are damaged, chest pain results. The coronary arteries may be damaged by arteriosclerosis, the most common cause. Angina pectoris is usually first treated with drugs, but if the condition worsens, coronary-artery bypass surgery (angioplasty) may need to be performed.

anorexia means a loss of appetite. Anorexia nervosa is a psychological disorder that is commonly associated with young females. The person has a false and distorted image of herself as fat and a fear, or phobia, relating to obesity, and becomes unable to eat. The person may take laxatives and induce vomiting, as well as starving herself, in order to lose weight.

antacids substances that neutralize acidity, usually hydrochloric acid in the digestive juices of the stomach. An example is sodium bicarbonate.

antibodies protein substances of the globulin type, which are produced by the lymphoid tissue and circulate in the blood. They react with their corresponding antigens and neutralize them, rendering them harmless. Antibodies are produced against a wide variety of antigens, and these reactions are responsible for immunity and allergy.

anticoagulants drugs or substances that delay or tend to prevent blood clotting, examples of which are warfarin and heparin. These are used in the treatment of embolism and thrombosis to disperse blood clots in vessels.

antigens any substances that cause the formation by the body of antibodies to neutralize their effect. Antigens are often protein substances, regarded as 'foreign' and 'invading' by the body, and elicit the production of antibodies against them.

antioxidants these are substances that react with free radicals and neutralize them, stopping cell damage. They include vitamins A, C, E, B_1 (thiamin), B_3 (niacin), B_5 (pantothenic acid), B_6 (pyroxidine), beta-carotene, as well as selenium, zinc, manganese and ubiquinone (co-enzyme Q10). The human body contains natural antioxidant enzymes as well, e.g. superoxide dismutase (SOD) and glutathione peroxidase.

apathy a condition where emotions, concern, passion and feelings are absent or suppressed. There is an indifference to stimuli that are normally moving or exciting.

arrhythmia any disturbance in the normal rhythm of heartbeat. The built-in pacemaker of the heart is the sino-atrial node situated in the wall of the right atrium, which itself is regulated by the autonomic nervous system. The electrical impulses produced by the pacemaker control the rate and rhythm of heartbeat. Arrhythmias occur when these electrical impulses are disturbed, and there are various different types. Most heart diseases cause arrhythmias, but they may also arise for no obvious cause.

arteriosclerosis a term used to describe several degenerative conditions affecting the arteries. The most common condition is known as hardening of the arteries. Fats, cholesterol, blood platelets and blood cells accumulate on the inside of the artery wall to form a plaque. This builds up over time and causes the blood vessel to constrict and limits the blood flow through the artery. This process is normally involved in myocardial infarction.

arthritis inflammation of the joints or spine, the symptoms of which are pain and swelling, restriction of movement, redness and warmth of the skin.

aspirin a type of drug in widespread use that is correctly called acetylsalicylic acid. It is used to relieve mild pain, e.g. headache, neuralgia and that associated with rheumatoid arthritis. It is also used to combat fever, and is also helpful in the prevention of coronary thrombosis. In susceptible individuals it may cause irritation and bleeding of the stomach lining, and is not normally given to children under the age of 12 years. High doses will cause dizziness and possibly mental confusion.

asthma a condition, characterized by breathing difficulties, caused by narrowing of the airways of the lung. It is a distressing condition, with breathlessness and a paroxysmal wheezing cough, and the extent to which the bronchi narrow varies considerably. Asthma may occur at any age but usually begins in early childhood, and is a hypersensitive response that can be brought on by exposure to a variety of allergens, exercise, stress or infections. An asthma sufferer may have other hypersensitive conditions, such as eczema and hay fever, and it may be prevalent within a family. It may or may not be possible for a person to avoid the allergen(s) responsible for an asthma attack. Treatment involves the use of drugs to dilate the airways (bronchodilators) and also inhaled corticosteroids.

astringent a substance that causes cells to contract by losing proteins from their surface. They cause localized contraction of blood vessels and are applied to minor wounds of the skin, and are used in mouth washes and eye drops.

atopic name given to conditions that develop because of an allergy, e.g. asthma, atopic dermatitis. It occurs because of the presence of an antibody (atopic reagin) in the skin or bloodstream.

auto-immune disease one of a number of conditions resulting from the production of antibodies by the body, which attack its own tissues. For reasons that are not understood the immune system loses the ability to distinguish between 'self' and 'nonself'. Auto-immune disease is currently thought to be the cause of a number of disorders, including acquired haemolytic anaemia.

Band III a transmembrane protein found in red blood cells of rats, rabbits, humans and several fish species. It allows chloride ions through to move across the red blood cell membrane, which is necessary for the formation of bicarbonate ions (CO_3^-) from carbon dioxide in the tissues. The bicarbonate is transported in the red blood cells from the tissues to the lungs, where the process is reversed and CO_2 is produced. This gas diffuses through the red blood cell membrane and the lung tissue into the air sacs of the lungs, from where it is exhaled. Band III is essential for respiration and forms part of the red blood cell's internal skeleton and so helps to maintain the cell's shape.

benign describes a disorder or condition that does not have any harmful effects. It is normally applied to a tumour that is not cancerous, or that does not invade or destroy the tissue where it develops, and does not spread to other sites in the body.

benzaldehyde C_7H_6O this chemical forms part of amygdalin, vitamin B_{17}. It is produced by the breakdown of this vitamin in the body and is not harmful to the tissues.

beriberi a disease caused by a dietary lack of vitamin B_1 (thiamin), which results in inflammation of the nerves, fever, paralysis and palpitations, and can occasionally precipitate heart failure. Beriberi is most prevalent in south-east Asia, China and Japan because of the removal of rice husks in processing.

beta blocker drugs used to treat angina, reduce high blood pressure and manage abnormal heart rhythms. Certain receptors of nerves in the sympathetic nervous system are blocked, reducing heart activity.

bile a viscous, bitter fluid produced by the liver and stored in the gall bladder, a small organ near the liver. It is an alkaline solution of bile salts, pigments, some mineral salts and cholesterol, which aids in fat digestion and absorption of nutrients. Discharge of bile into the intestine is increased after food, and of the amount secreted each day (up to one litre), most is re-absorbed with the food, passing back into the blood to circulate back to the liver. If the flow of bile into the intestine is restricted, it stays in the blood, resulting in jaundice.

bioavailability the term used to describe the amount of a drug that becomes available at its target, after administration and having followed a particular route. The amount may be low for drugs administered by mouth since food affects bioavailability through the alteration of the rate of absorption. Components of food, e.g. calcium, may act as a chelating agent (restricting the amount of the drug that is free), also reducing the absorption of a drug.

blood a suspension of red blood cells (or corpuscles) called erythrocytes, white blood cells (leucocytes) and platelets (small disc-shaped cells involved in blood clotting) in a liquid medium, blood plasma. The circulation of blood through the body provides a mechanism for transporting substances. Its functions include:

(1) carrying oxygenated blood from the heart to all tissues via the arteries while the veins return deoxygenated blood to the heart.

(2) carrying essential nutrients, e.g. glucose, fats and amino acids, to all parts of the body.

(3) removing the waste products of metabolism—ammonia and carbon dioxide—to the liver, where urea is formed and then transported by the blood to the kidneys for excretion.

(4) carrying important molecules, e.g. hormones, to their target cells.

The red blood cells, produced in the bone marrow, are haemoglobin-containing discs while the white varieties vary in shape and are produced in the marrow and lymphoid tissue. The plasma comprises water, proteins and electrolytes and forms approximately half the blood volume.

blood-brain barrier this is a semipermeable membrane that separates the brain and cerebrospinal fluids from the blood. It permits the solutions, small molecules or lipid soluble molecules to pass through it but excludes large molecules and solid material. It prevents the movement of certain drugs into the brain and this can be difficult if treating diseases such as Parkinson's disease.

blood clot a hard mass of blood platelets, trapped red blood cells and fibrin. After tissue damage, blood vessels in the area are constricted and a plug forms to seal the damaged area. The plug formation is initiated by an enzyme released by the damaged blood vessels and platelets.

blood plasma the fluid that bathes the platelets, red blood cells and the white blood cells. It is a solution of several inorganic salts, trace substances and proteins including the coagulating factors, e.g. fibrinogens.

blood serum this fluid is similar to plasma but lacks all the coagulating factors including fibrinogen.

blood vessel the veins and arteries and their smaller branchings, venules and arterioles, through which blood is carried to and from the heart.

bone the hard connective tissue that with cartilage forms the skeleton. Bone has a matrix of collagen fibres with bone salts (crystalline calcium phosphate or hydroxyapatite, in which are the bone cells, osteoblasts and osteocytes). The bone cells form the matrix.

There are two types of bone: compact or dense, forming the shafts of long bones, and spongy or cancellous, which occurs on the inside and at the ends of long bones and also forms the short bones. Compact bone is a hard tube covered by the periosteum (a membrane) and enclosing the marrow and contains very fine canals around which the bone is structured in circular plates.

bone marrow a soft tissue found in the spaces of bones. In young animals all bone marrow, the red marrow, produces blood cells. In older animals the marrow in long bones is replaced by yellow marrow, which contains a large amount of fat and does not produce blood cells. In mature animals the red marrow occurs in the ribs, sternum, vertebrae and the ends of the long bones (e.g. the femur). The red marrow contains myeloid tissue with erythroblasts from which red blood cells develop. Leucocytes also form from the myeloid tissue and themselves give rise to other cell types.

calcification the deposition of calcium salts that is normal in the formation of bone but may occur at other sites in the body.

calculus the formation of a stone in the body, particularly in the gallbladder and in the urinary tract. They can cause considerable pain if sited in a tissue or in a duct, e.g. the ureter. They are composed of mineral salts such as calcium oxalate.

cancer a widely used term describing any form of malignant tumour. Characteristically, there is an uncontrolled and abnormal growth of cancer cells that invade surrounding tissues and destroy them. Cancer cells may spread throughout the body via the blood stream or lymphatic system, a process known as metastasis, and set up secondary growths elsewhere. There are known to be a number of different causes of cancer including cigarette smoking, radiation, ultraviolet light, some viruses and possibly the presence of cancer genes (oncogenes). Treatment depends upon the site of the cancer but involves radiotherapy, chemotherapy and surgery, and survival rates in affected people are showing encouraging improvements. Vitamin and mineral supplements are currently used as adjuvant therapy to help ease the side effects of chemotherapy and radiotherapy.

capillary a fine blood vessel that communicates with an arteriole or venule. Capillaries form networks in most tissues and have walls that are only one cell thick. There is a constant exchange of substances (oxygen, carbon dioxide, nutrients, etc) between the capillaries, arterioles and venules supplying the needs of the surrounding tissues.

carbohydrates organic compounds that include sugars and starch and contain carbon, hydrogen and oxygen. They are the most important source of energy available to the body and are an essential part of the diet. They are eventually broken down in the body to the simple sugar, glucose, which can be used by cells in numerous metabolic processes.

carcinogen any substance that causes damage to tissue cells likely to result in cancer. Various substances are known to be *carcinogenic* including tobacco smoke, asbestos and ionizing radiation.

cardiac arrest the failure and stopping of the pumping action of the heart. There is a loss of consciousness and breathing and the pulse ceases. Death follows very rapidly unless the heart beat can be restored, and methods of achieving this include external cardiac massage, artificial respiration, defibrillation and direct cardiac massage.

cardiac muscle specialized muscle unique to the heart, consisting of branching, elongated fibres possessing the ability to contract and relax continuously.

cartilage a type of firm connective tissue that is pliable and forms part of the skeleton. There are three different kinds, hyaline cartilage, fibrocartilage and elastic cartilage. *Hyaline* cartilage is found at the joints of movable bones and in the trachea, nose, bronchi and as costal cartilage joining the ribs to the breast bone. *Fibrocartilage*, which consists of cartilage and connective tissue, is found in the intervertebral discs of the spinal column and in tendons. *Elastic* cartilage is found in the external part of the ear (pinna).

catabolism the biochemical processes within the body (metabolism) are divided into two different sorts—those that build up or produce (synthesize) substances, which is anabolism, and those which break down material (lysis), known as catabolism. In catabolism, more complex materials are broken down into simpler ones with a release of energy, as occurs during the digestion of food.

catalase an enzyme that is found in nearly all body cells. It catalyses the process where hydrogen peroxide (H_2O_2) is decomposed into water and oxygen.

celiac disease (*or* **gluten allergy**) this is a metabolic disorder, which means the person cannot break down peptides in gluten. Symptoms include vomiting, diarrhoea, abdominal distention, muscle wasting and extreme lethargy. The disease can be resolved by eating a high-calorie, high-protein diet that is free of gluten.

cheiosis a condition where the lips and mouth are bright red in colour, swollen and cracked. It occurs because of many nutritional disorders including a deficiency of riboflavin, vitamin B_2.

chelate this is a salt formed when a metal ion is enclosed in an organic ring molecule. Chelation is the reaction that occurs when a metal and a chelating agent combine to form a ring-shaped molecular complex. Chelate salts of gold are occasionally used to treat some medical conditions.

chemotherapy the treatment of disease by the administration of chemical substances or drugs. It includes the treatment of infectious diseases with antibiotics and other types of drug. Also the treatment and control of various tropical diseases and, especially in recent years, many different forms of cancer with antimetabolite drugs.

cholesterol a fatty insoluble molecule (sterol) that is widely found in the body and is synthesized from saturated fatty acids in the liver. Cholesterol is an important substance in the body being a component of cell membranes and a precursor in the production of steroid hormones (sex hormones) and bile salts. An elevated level of blood cholesterol is associated with development of arteriosclerosis, which may result in high blood pressure and coronary thrombosis, and this is seen in the disease, diabetes mellitus. There appears to be a relationship between the high consumption of saturated animal fats (which contain cholesterol) in the western diet and the greater incidence of coronary heart disease among, for example, Western Europeans and North Americans. It is generally recommended that people in these countries should reduce their consumption of saturated fat and look for alternatives in the form of unsaturated fats, which are found in vegetable oils.

cholesterol-HDL this is a plasma protein involved in transporting cholesterol and other lipids from the blood plasma to the tissues. It has a different composition to LDL cholesterol and has a protective function by removing excess cholesterol from the blood and so reducing the incidence of heart disease and arteriosclerosis.

cholesterol-LDL cholesterol is carried in the blood by carrier molecules called high or low-density lipoproteins. LDL-cholesterol is removed from the blood via LDL-receptors on the plasma membrane of cells, and the cells take up the cholesterol. This helps to regulate the levels of cholesterol in the blood. Unfortunately LDL-cholesterol leaves any excess cholesterol in the blood where it can permeate the walls of the arteries and start the development of arteriosclerosis. So elevated levels of cholesterol in the blood are dangerous to human health and we should try to maintain a higher level of the beneficial HDL-cholesterol in our blood as it reduces the risk of disease arising.

choline an organic compound that is a constituent of some important substances in the body such as phospholipids, lecithin and acetycholine. It is sometimes classed as part of the vitamin B complex but this essential compound can also be synthesized by the body.

chromosomes the rodlike structures, present in the nucleus of every body cell, that carry the genetic information, or genes. Each human body cell contains twenty-three pairs of chromosomes (apart from the sperm and ova), half derived from the mother and half from the father. Each chromosome consists of a coiled double filament (double helix) of DNA with genes carrying the genetic information arranged linearly along its length. The genes determine all the characteristics of each individual. Twenty-two of the pairs of chromosomes are the same in males and females. The twenty-third pair are the sex chromosomes and males have one X and one Y whereas females have two X chromosomes.

chronic describing a disease that develops slowly and persists for a long period of time. Onset of disease is often gradual and it may remain for the whole of a person's lifetime.

chyme the partly digested food that passes from the stomach into the intestine. It is produced by the mechanical movements of the stomach and the acid secretions present in the gastric juice.

cirrhosis a disease of the liver in which fibrous tissue resembling scar tissue is produced as a result of damage and death to the cells. The liver becomes yellow-coloured and nodular in appearance, and there are various types of the disease including alcoholic cirrhosis and postnecrotic cirrhosis caused by viral hepatitis. The cause of the cirrhosis is not always found (cryptogenic cirrhosis) but the progress of the condition can be halted if this can be identified and removed. This particularly is applicable in alcoholic cirrhosis where the consumption of alcohol has to cease.

cleft palate a developmental defect in which a fissure is left in the mid-line of the palate as the two sides fail to fuse. It may also involve the lip (harelip) and the condition is corrected by surgery.

coagulation (of the blood) the natural process in which blood is converted from a liquid to a semisolid state to arrest bleeding (haemorrhage). A substance known as prothrombin and calcium are normally present in the blood, and the enzyme thromboplastin is present in the platelets. When bleeding occurs, thromboplastin is released and prothrombin and calcium are converted by the enzyme into thrombin. A soluble protein, called fibrinogen, is always present in the blood and is converted by thrombin into fibrin, which is the final stage in the coagulation process. A fibrous mesh or clot is produced, consisting of fibrin and blood cells, which seals off the damaged blood vessel. In normal healthy conditions, thromboplastin is not released and so a clot cannot form. The coagulation or clotting time is the time taken for blood to clot and is normally between three to eight minutes.

co-enzymes these are non-protein organic compounds that are required in association with an enzyme to catalyse biochemical reactions. Co-enzymes normally function by donating or accepting various chemical groups. Many co-enzymes are derived from vitamins, e.g. lipoic acid, vitamin B_3 (niacin), biotin (vitamin H) and pantothenic acid (vitamin B_5).

co-factor some enzymes can only work if their particular co-factor is present. Co-factors may be inorganic (e.g. metal ions) or non-protein organic substances (e.g. co-enzymes), and they may activate their enzyme or actually take part in the reaction itself.

colitis inflammation of the colon, the symptoms of which include abdominal pain and diarrhoea, sometimes bloodstained. *Ulcerative colitis* tends to affect young adults and tends to occur periodically over a number of years. There is abdominal discomfort, fever, frequent watery diarrhoea containing mucus and blood, and anaemia. The condition can be fatal but usually there is a gradual recovery. Treatment is by means of bed rest, drug treatment with corticosteroids and iron supplements, and a bland, low roughage diet.

collagen a protein substance that is widely found in large amounts in the body in connective tissue, tendons, skin, cartilage, bone and ligaments. It plays a major part in conferring tensile strength to various body structures.

complement a group of proteins found in the blood serum, which help defend the body from pathogens. They may attract phagocytic cells to the area of conflict and cause pathogenic cells to lyse, or rupture. Also act as chemical messengers for white blood cells.

compound a substance that is formed by the chemical reaction of two or more elements.

connective tissue supporting or packing tissue within the body, which holds or separates other tissues and organs. It consists of a ground material composed of substances called mucopolysaccharides. In this, certain fibres such as yellow elastic, white collagenous and reticular fibres are embedded along with a variety of other cells, e.g. mast cells, macrophages, fibroblasts and fat cells. The constituents vary in proportions in different kinds of connective tissue to produce a number of distinct types. Examples are adipose (fatty) tissue, cartilage, bone, tends and ligaments.

coronary arteries the arteries that supply blood to the heart and arise from the aorta.

coronary artery disease any abnormal condition that affects the arteries of the heart. The commonest disease is coronary atherosclerosis, which is more prevalent in those populations with high levels of saturated fat, refined carbohydrates, etc, in their diet. Angina is a common symptom of such diseases.

coronary thrombosis a sudden blockage of one of the coronary arteries by a blood clot or thrombus, which interrupts the blood supply to the heart. The victim collapses with severe and agonizing chest pain often accompanied by vomiting and nausea. The skin becomes pale and clammy, the temperature rises and there is difficulty in breathing. Coronary thrombosis generally results from atheroma, and the part of the heart muscle that has its blood supply disrupted dies, a condition known as myocardial infarction. Treatment consists of giving strong pain-relieving drugs such as morphine. Also specialist care in a coronary care unit is usually required to deal with arrhythmia, heart failure and cardiac arrest, which are the potentially fatal results of coronary thrombosis.

cramp prolonged and painful spasmodic muscular contraction that often occurs in the limbs but can affect certain internal organs. Cramp may result from a salt imbalance as in heat cramp. Working in high temperatures causes excessive sweating and consequent loss of salt. It can be corrected and prevented by an increase of the salt intake. Occupational cramp results from continual repetitive use of particular muscles, e.g. writer's cramp. Night cramp occurs during sleep and is especially common among elderly people, diabetics and pregnant women. The cause is not known.

cretinism a syndrome caused by lack of thyroid hormone, which is present before birth, and is also called *congenital hyperthyroidism*. It is characterized by dwarfism, mental retardation and coarseness of skin and hair. Early diagnosis and treatment with thyroxine is vital as this greatly improves a child's intellectual and other abilities. In the UK, blood serum from newborn babies is tested for thyroxine levels in order to detect this condition.

cross-linkage (*or* **crossing-over**) cross-linkage is a process that occurs during meiosis, a type of cell division that produces spermatozoa and eggs with half the normal number of chromosomes. Meiosis occurs in four stages and crossing-over mainly occurs at the end of the first stage. Crossing-over is the exchange of sections of chromatids between pairs of similar chromosomes. This means genetic material is recombined and the patterns of genes in the chromosome is altered. The process results in new genetic variation and forms chiasma (points of contact between chromosomes).

cytosol this is the living contents

of the cell excluding the cell organelles and other particles. It is composed of a solution of lipids, nucleic acids, proteins phospholipids along with many ions, e.g. calcium, magnesium. It also contains smaller molecules such as sugars, nucleotides and amino acids. The cytosol is the site of some enzymes processes and acts as a storage area for metabolites and enzymes.

cytotoxic a substance that damages or destroys cells. Cytotoxic drugs are used in the treatment of various forms of cancer and act by inhibiting cell division. However, they also damage normal cells and hence their use has to be carefully regulated in each individual patient. Cytotoxic drugs may be used in combination with radiotherapy or on their own.

degeneration the deterioration over time of body tissues or an organ resulting in a lessening of its function. The changes may be structural or chemical and there are a number of types: fatty, fibroid, calcareous, mucoid and so on. Degeneration may be caused by ageing, heredity or poor nutrition. Poisons such as alcohol also contribute to degeneration, as in cirrhosis.

depression a mental state of extreme sadness dominated by pessimism and in which normal behaviour patterns (sleep, appetite, etc) are disturbed. Causes are varied: upsetting events, loss, etc, and treatment involves the use of therapy and drugs.

dialysis the use of a semipermeable membrane to separate large and small molecules by selective diffusion. Starch and proteins are large molecules while salts, glucose and amino acids are small molecules. If a mixture of large and small molecules is separated from distilled water by a semipermeable membrane, the smaller molecules diffuse into the water, which is itself replenished. This principle is the basis of the artificial kidney, which, because a patient's blood is processed, is known as haemodialysis.

dietary reference values (DRVs) a term given to nutrient recommendation values (*see* EAR, LRNI, RDA, RNI).

diuretic a substance that increases urine formation and excretion and that may work specifically within the kidney, e.g. by prevention of sodium, and therefore water, re-absorption or outside the kidney.

DNA (deoxyribonucleic acid) a nucleic acid and the primary constituent of chromosomes. It transmits genetic information from parents to offspring in the form of genes. It is a very large molecule comprising two twisted nucleotide chains that can store enormous amounts of information in a stable but not rigid way i.e. parental traits and characteristics are passed on but evolutionary changes are allowed to occur.

dosage the overall amount of a drug administered, determined by size, frequency and number of doses and taking into account the patient's age, weight and possible allergic reactions. Modern techniques enable controlled dosage using transdermals (drugs absorbed from a plaster on the skin) and implantable devices.

Duchenne's muscular dystrophy this disease is genetically transmitted to an X-chromosome. It arises between 3 and 5 years of age and causes progressive wasting of the muscles in the legs and pelvis. The disease progresses to cause a waddling gait and lordosis, generally leading to death by the early twenties. Some women only have one copy of the gene for the disease and are termed carriers. Tests can now be done to detect people carrying the gene and so try to reduce the incidence of the disease. This is the most common form of muscular dystrophy.

dyslexia a disorder that renders reading or learning to read difficult. There is usually an associated problem in writing and spelling correctly. A very small number of children are affected severely and boys are more prone than girls by a factor of three.

eczema an inflammation of the skin that causes itching, a red rash and often small blisters that weep and become encrusted. This may be followed by the skin thickening and then peeling off in scales. There are several types of eczema, *atopic* being one of the most common. (Atopic is the hereditary tendency to form allergic reactions because of an antibody in the skin). A form of atopic eczema is infantile eczema that starts at 3 or 4 months and it is often the case that eczema, hay fever and asthma is found in the family history. However, many children improve markedly as they approach the age of 10 or 11. The treatment for such conditions usually involves the use of hydrocortisone and other steroid creams and ointments.

electrocardiogram a record of the changes in the heart's electrical potential, on an instrument called an electrocardiograph. The subject is connected to the equipment by leads on the chest and legs or arms. A normal trace has one wave for the activity of the atria and others relating to the ventricular beat. Abnormal heart activity is often indicated in the trace and it therefore forms a useful diagnostic aid.

electron transport chain a sequence of enzymes and proteins that transfer electrons or hydrogen atoms along the chain in a series of oxidation-reduction reactions and so produce energy. This occurs in the mitochondria of human cells and involves flavoproteins such as flavin adenine dinucleotide (FAD), flavin mononucleotide (FMN), nicotinamide adenine dinucleotide (NAD), cytochromes and ubiquinone (co-enzyme Q10). Most of these chemicals are made from vitamins such as riboflavin (vitamin B_2) and niacin (vitamin B_3).

emaciation particularly severe leanness caused by lack of nourishment or disease. It tends to be associated with diseases such as tuberculosis or diseases producing diarrhoea over a long period of time.

endocrine glands ductless glands that produce hormones for secretion directly into the bloodstream (or lymph). Some organs, e.g. the pancreas, also release secretions via a duct. In addition to the pancreas the major endocrine glands are the thyroid, pituitary, parathyroid, ovary and testis. Imbalances in the secretions of endocrine glands produce a variety of diseases.

endometriosis the occurrence of endometrium in other parts of the body, e.g. within the muscle of the uterus, in the ovary, Fallopian tubes, peritoneum and possibly the bowel. Because of the nature of tissue, it acts in a way similar to that of the uterus lining and causes pelvic pain, bleeding, painful menstruation. The condition occurs between puberty and the menopause and ceases during pregnancy. The treatment required may include total hysterectomy, but occasionally the administration of a steroid hormone will alleviate the symptoms.

enzyme any protein molecule that acts as a catalyst in the biochemical processes of the body. They are essential to life and are highly specific, acting on certain substrates at a set temperature and pH. Examples are the digestive enzymes amylase, lipase and trypsin. Enzymes act by providing active sites (one or more for each enzyme) to which substrate molecules bind, forming a short-lived intermediate. The rate of reaction is increased, and after the product is formed, the active site is freed. Enzymes are easily rendered inactive by heat and some chemicals. The names of most enzymes end in *-ase*, and this is added onto the name of the substrate thus a peptidase breaks down peptides. Enzymes are vital for the normal functioning of the body and their lack or inactivity can produce metabolic disorders.

epilepsy a neurological disorder involving convulsions, seizures and loss of consciousness. There are many possible causes or associations of epilepsy, including cerebral trauma, brain tumour, cerebral haemorrhage and metabolic imbalances as in hypoglycaemia. Usually an epileptic attack occurs without warning, with complete unconsciousness and some muscle contraction and spasms. Some drugs are used in treatment although little can be done during the fit itself.

erythrocyte the red blood cell that is made in the bone marrow and occurs as a red disc, concave on both sides, full of haemoglobin. These cells are responsible for carrying oxygen to tissues and carbon dioxide away The latter is removed in the form of the bicarbonate ion (HCO_3^-), in exchange for a chloride ion (Cl^-). There are approximately five million erythrocytes in one millilitre of blood and they are active for about 120 days before being absorbed by macrophages.

essential amino acid of the twenty amino acids required by the body, a number are termed essential because they must be in the diet as they cannot be synthesized in the body. The essential ones are: isoleucine, leucine, lysine, methionine, phenylalanine, threonine, tryptophan and valine. In addition, infants require arginine and histidine. A lack leads to protein deficiency, but they are available in meat, cheese and eggs, and all eight would be obtained if the diet contained corn and beans.

essential fatty acid there are three polyunsaturated acids in this category, which cannot be produced in the body—arachidonic, linoleic and linolenic. These compounds are found in vegetable and fish oils and are vital in metabolism and proper functioning of the body. A deficiency may cause such symptoms as allergic conditions, skin disorders, poor hair and nails and so on.

estimated average requirement (EAR) this is the average requirement for a nutrient in the human diet.

excreta waste material discharged

from the body. The term is often used specifically to denote faeces.

excretion the removal of all waste material from the body, including urine and faeces, the loss of water and salts through sweat glands, and the elimination of carbon dioxide and water vapour from the lungs.

fatigue physical or mental tiredness following a prolonged period of hard work. Muscle fatigue resulting from hard exercise is caused by a build up of *lactic acid.* Lactic acid is produced in muscles (as an end product of the breakdown of glycogen to produce energy), and builds up when there is an insufficient supply of oxygen. The muscle is unable to work properly until a period of rest and restored oxygen supply enables the lactic acid to be removed.

fatty acids a group of organic compounds each consisting of a long, straight hydrocarbon chain and a terminal carboxylic acid (COOH) group. The length of the chain varies from one to nearly thirty carbon atoms and the chains may be *saturated* or *unsaturated.* Some fatty acids can be synthesized within the body but others, the essential fatty acids, must be obtained from food. Fatty acids have three major roles within the body: (1) They are components of glycolipids (lipids containing carbohydrate) and phospholipids (lipids containing phosphate). These are of major importance in the structure of tissues and organs.
(2) Fatty acids are important constituents of triglycerides (lipids that have three fatty acid molecules joined to a glycerol molecule). They are stored in the cytoplasm of many cells and are broken down when required to yield energy. They are the form in which the body stores fat. (3) Derivatives of fatty acids function as hormones and intracellular messengers.

fever an elevation of body temperature above the normal, which accompanies many diseases and infections. The cause of fever is the production by the body of pyrogen, which acts on the thermoregulatory centre in the hypothalamus of the brain. This responds by promoting mechanisms that increase heat generation and lessen heat loss, leading to a rise in temperature. Fever is the main factor in many infections caused by bacteria or viruses and results from toxins produced by the growth of these organisms. Examples of these *primary* or *specific* fevers are diphtheria, scarlet fever and typhoid fever. An *intermittent fever* describes a fluctuating body temperature, which commonly accompanies malaria, in which the temperature sometimes returns to normal. Treatment of fever depends upon the underlying cause. However, it may be necessary to reduce the temperature by direct methods such as sponging the body with tepid water, or by giving drugs such as aspirin. As well as a rise in body temperature, symptoms of fever include headache, shivering, nausea, diarrhoea or constipation. Above 105°F, there may be delirium or convulsions, especially in young children.

fibrin the end product of the process of blood coagulation, comprising threads of insoluble protein formed from a soluble precursor, fibrinogen, by the activity of the enzyme thrombin. Fibrin forms a network that is the basis of a blood clot.

fibrinogen a coagulation factor present in the blood, which is a soluble protein and the precursor of fibrin.

flavoprotein a group of proteins where a derivative of riboflavin (vitamin B_2) is bound to a protein as a prosethic group. The flavin derivatives are flavin adenine dinucleotide (FAD) and flavin mononucleotide (FMN) and they allow the flavoproteins to act as important enzymes in the electron transport chain.

free radicals these are chemicals that have one or more unpaired electrons in their outer shell. This makes them highly reactive. They are normally produced in our body as they are needed for body functions, but uncontrolled production of free radicals is dangerous as they can attack and destroy cells. Oxygen free radicals and hydrogen peroxide are some of the most common examples. (*See* section in text).

Friedreich's ataxia an inherited disorder caused by degeneration of nerve cells in the brain and spinal cord. It appears in children, usually in adolescence, and the symptoms include unsteadiness during walking and a loss of the knee-jerk reflex, leading progressively to tremors, speech impairment and curvature of the spine. The symptoms are increasingly disabling and may be accompanied by heart disease.

gamete a mature germ or sexual cell, male or female, that can participate in fertilization, e.g. ovum and spermatozoa.

gene the fundamental unit of genetic material found at a specific location on a chromosome. It is chemically complex and responsible for the transmission of information between older and younger generations. Each gene contributes to a particular trait or characteristic. There are more than 100,000 genes in man and gene size varies with the characteristic, e.g. the gene that codes for the hormone insulin is 1700 base pairs long.

There are several types of gene, depending upon their function, and in addition genes are said to be dominant or recessive. A dominant characteristic is one that occurs whenever the gene is present, while the effect of a recessive gene (say a disease) requires that the gene be on both members of the chromosome pair, i.e. it must be homozygous.

genetic code specific information carried by DNA molecules that controls the particular amino acids and their positions in every protein and thus all the proteins synthesized within a cell. Because there are just four nucleotides a unit of three bases becomes the smallest unit that can produce codes for all 20 amino acids. The transfer of information from gene to protein is based upon three consecutive nucleotides called *codons*. A change in the genetic code results in an amino acid being inserted incorrectly in a protein, resulting in a mutation.

gland an organ or group of cells that secretes a specific substance or substances. Endocrine glands secrete directly into the blood while *exocrine* glands secrete onto an epithelial surface via a duct. Some glands produce fluids, e.g. milk from the mammary glands, saliva from the sublingual gland, and others. The thyroid gland is an endocrine gland releasing hormones into the bloodstream. A further system of glands, the lymphatic glands, occur throughout the body in association with the lymphatic vessels

globulin a group of globular proteins that occur widely in milk, blood, eggs and plants. There are four types in blood serum: a_1, a_2, b, and g. The alpha and beta types are carrier proteins like haemoglobin and gamma globulins include the immunoglobulins involved in the immune response.

gluconeogenesis the formation of glucose from pyruvate, derived from fat, protein and lactose molecules. This occurs mainly in the liver and takes place by reversing the reactions in glycolysis. It is stimulated by several hormones found in the body including adrenaline, cortisol, thyroxine and growth hormone.

glycogen sometimes called **animal starch**, is a carbohydrate (polysaccharide) stored mainly in the liver. It acts as an energy store that is liberated upon hydrolysis.

glycolysis a series of biochemical reactions by which glucose is broken down to pyruvate, releasing energy. This is the first leg of energy production from dietary foodstuffs and the pyruvate is passed on to the Krebs cycle. When oxygen is in short supply, e.g. during exercise, the pyruvate may be converted into other chemicals such as lactic acid, by anaerobic respiration. This lactic acid builds up in the muscles and causes cramps. Glycolysis is mostly a reversible process and the reformation of glucose from pyruvate is called gluconeogenesis.

glycoside a group of crystalline, bitter substances where a sugar derivative is bound to an organic group.

goitre swelling of the neck caused by thyroid gland enlargement. The thyroid tries to counter the dietary lack of iodine necessary to produce thyroid hormone, by increasing the output, thereby becoming larger. The endemic or simple goitre is due to this cause. Other types are caused by hyperplasia and auto-immune diseases, for example when antibodies are produced against antigens in the thyroid gland.

gold salts (*or* **gold compound**) chemicals containing gold that are used in minute quantities to treat rheumatoid arthritis. It is given by injection into muscles and because side effects may include skin reactions, blood disorders, mouth ulcers and inflammation of the kidneys, very careful control is kept on the dosage.

Grave's disease a disorder typified by thyroid gland over-activity , an enlargement of the gland, and protruding eyes. It is caused by antibody production and is probably an auto-immune response . Patients commonly exhibit excess metabolism (because thyroid hormones control the body's metabolism); nervousness, tremor, hyperactivity, rapid heart rate, an intolerance of heat, breathlessness and so on. Treatment may follow one of three courses; drugs to control the thyroid's production of hormones; surgery to remove part of the thyroid; or radioactive iodine therapy.

haem a compound containing iron, composed of a pigment, known as a *porphyrin*, which confers colour. It combines with a protein called globin in the blood to form haemoglobin. The prefix *haem* also indicates anything relating to blood.

haemochromatosis a disorder

where there is excessive absorption and storage of iron in the body. Symptoms include bronze coloration of the skin, liver failure and diabetes. Iron deposits are found throughout the body and may damage the functioning of the pancreas, liver and endocrine glands. The excess iron is removed by taking blood or by administering an iron chelating agent so the iron is eliminated via the excreta.

haemoglobin the respiratory substance contained within the red blood cells, which contains a pigment responsible for the red colour of blood. It consists of the pigment haem and the protein globin and is responsible for the transport of oxygen around the body. Oxygen is picked up in the lungs by arterial blood and transported to the tissues where it is released. This (venous) blood is then returned to the lungs to repeat the process.

haemosiderosis a condition where excess iron is deposited in the tissues, normally as haemosiderin. This does not usually result in tissue damage but may harm the heart and liver on occasions. The excess iron may derive from excessive levels of intake, particularly from blood transfusions.

hare lip a congenital developmental deformity that results in the presence of a cleft in the upper lip. It is brought about by a failure in the fusion of three blocks of embryonic tissue and is often associated with a cleft palate.

hay fever an allergic reaction to pollen, e.g. that of grasses, trees and many other plants, which affects numerous individuals. The symptoms are a blocked and runny nose, sneezing and watering eyes caused by the release of histamine. Treatment is by means of antihistamine drugs and, if the allergen can be identified, *desensitization* may be successful. This involves injecting or exposing the individual to controlled and gradually increasing doses of the allergen until antibodies are built up.

headache pain felt within the head, which is thought to be caused by dilation of intracranial arteries or pressure upon them. Common causes are stress, tiredness, feverishness accompanying an infection such as a cold, an excess of close work involving the eyes, dyspepsia, rheumatic diseases, high blood pressure and uraemia. Headache may indicate the presence of disease or disorder in the brain.

heart the hollow, muscular organ that acts as a pump and is responsible for the circulation of the blood. The heart is cone-shaped with the point downwards and is situated between the lungs and slightly to the left of the mid-line. The heart projects forwards and lies beneath the fifth rib. The wall consists mainly of cardiac muscle lined on the inside by a membrane known as the endocardium. An external membrane known as the pericardium surrounds the heart. A septum divides the heart into right and left halves, each of which is further divided into an upper chamber known as an atrium and a lower one called a ventricle. Four valves control the direction of blood flow at each outlet, comprising the aortic, pulmonary, tricuspid and mitral (bicuspid). These valves prevent back-flow once the blood has been forced from one chamber into the next.

histamine a substance derived from histidine, which is an amino acid. It is widely found throughout all the body tissues and is responsible for the dilation of blood vessels (arterioles and capillaries) and the contraction of smooth muscle, including that of the bronchi of the lungs. Histamine is released in great quantities in allergic conditions and anaphylaxis (*see also* allergy).

Hodgkin's disease a malignant disease of unknown cause affecting the lymphatic system in which there is a gradual and increasing enlargement of lymph glands and nodes throughout the body. The accompanying symptoms include loss of weight, sweating, anaemia and a characteristic type of fever (known as Pel-Ebstein fever). The person becomes gradually weaker and the glands may attain a very large size. The outlook is good, especially if the disease is detected early, and treatment is by means of surgery, radiotherapy and chemotherapy (with a combination of drugs) one or more of these being employed.

homeostatis the process that maintains the internal systems of the body, e.g. heartbeat, blood pressure, body temperature and respiration at equilibrium, despite the varying conditions outside the body.

hormone a naturally produced chemical substance produced by the body, which acts as a messenger. A hormone is produced by cells or glands in one part of the body and passes into the bloodstream. When it reaches another specific site, its 'target organ', it causes a reaction there, modifying the structure or function of cells, perhaps by causing the release of another hormone.

Hormones are secreted by the endocrine glands and examples are the sex hormones, e.g. testosterone secreted by the testes and oestradiol and progesterone secreted by the ovaries.

hydrogen cyanide a very powerful poison that is released inside cells when amygdalin (vitamin B_{17}) is broken down.

hydroxocobalamin this is a cobalt-containing (cobalamin) substance used in the treatment of vitamin B_{12} deficiencies, such as pernicious anaemia.

hypersensitivity abnormal allergic response to an antigen to which the person has previously been exposed. Hypersensitive responses vary from quite mild such as hay fever to very severe and life-threatening, e.g. anaphylactic shock (*see also* allergy).

hypertension high blood pressure (in the arteries). *Essential* hypertension may be due to an unknown cause, or kidney disease or endocrine diseases. *Malignant* hypertension will prove fatal if not treated. It may be a condition itself or an end stage of essential hypertension. It tends to occur in a younger age group and there is high diastolic blood pressure and kidney failure. Previously a rapidly fatal condition, antihypertensive drugs have revolutionized treatment and given sufferers a near-normal life.

hyperthyroidism excessive activity of the thyroid gland—an over-active thyroid. It may be caused by increased growth of the gland, by the presence of a tumour or because of graves disease.

hypoglycaemia a condition that develops because of a blood glucose level that is less than normal. It may occur because of too much insulin or dietary deficiency and symptoms include headache, hunger, weakness, anxiety and visual disturbances.

ileum the lower part of the small intestine between the jejunum and the caecum.

ileus an obstruction of the intestine (often the ileum), which may be mechanical, caused by worms or a gallstone from the gall bladder, or which can be caused by the loss of the natural movement of the intestines (peristalsis). This latter condition may be caused by surgery, injury to the spine, or peritonitis.

immunity the way in which the body resists infection because of the presence of antibodies and white blood cells. Antibodies are generated in response to the presence of antigens of a disease. There are several types of immunity: *active immunity* is when the body produces antibodies and continues to be able to do so, during the course of a disease whether occurring naturally (also called *acquired immunity*) or by deliberate stimulation. *Passive immunity* is shortlived and caused by the injection of ready-made antibodies from someone who is already immune.

immunization the process of producing immunity to disease by artificial means. Injection of an antiserum will produce temporary passive immunity. Active immunity is produced by making the body generate its own antibodies, and this is done by the use of treated antigens (vaccination or inoculation). Vaccine is used for immunization, and it may be made of treated live bacteria or viruses or dead organisms or their products.

immunoglobulins a group of high molecular weight proteins that act as antibodies and are present in the serum and secretions. Designated Ig, there are five groups, each with different functions identified by a particular letter: Immunoglobulin A (Ig A) is the most common and occurs in all secretions of the body. It is the main antibody in the mucous membrane of the intestines, bronchi, saliva and tears. It defends the body against microorganisms by combining with a protein in the mucosa.

Ig D is found in the serum in small amounts but increases during allergic reactions.

Ig E is found primarily in the lungs, skin and mucous membrane cells and is an anaphylactic antibody.

Ig G is synthesized to combat bacteria and viruses in the body. Ig M (or macroglobulin) has a very high molecular weight (about five or six times that of the others) and is the first produced by the body when antigens occur. It is also the main antibody in blood group incompatibilities.

induration this is the hardening of a tissue because of oedema, inflammation or cancer. Induration of the muscles in the leg is a symptom of severe scurvy, which develops because of insufficient vitamin C.

infarction the formation of an *infarct* or dead area of tissue in an organ or vessel because of the obstruction of the artery supplying blood. The obstruction may be caused by a blood clot or an embolus.

inflammation the response of the body's tissues to injury, which involves pain, redness, heat and swelling (*acute* inflammation). The first sign when the tissues are infected or injured physically or chemically is a dilation of blood vessels in the affected area increasing blood flow resulting in heat and redness. The circulation then slows a little and white blood cells migrate into the tissues producing the swelling. The white blood cells engulf invading bacteria, dead tissue, foreign particles. After this either the white blood cells migrate back to the circulation, or there is the production and discharge of pus, as healing commences. *Chronic* inflammation is when repair is not complete and there is formation of scar tissue.

ingestion the process of chewing and swallowing food and fluid, which then go into the stomach. Also the means whereby a *phagocyte* (a cell that can surround and break down cell debris, foreign particles and microorganisms) takes in particles.

inorganic compound this is a range of compounds that do not contain carbon.

insomnia being unable to remain asleep or to fall asleep in the first instance, resulting in debilitating tiredness. It may be caused by a painful condition but is more likely to be caused by anxiety.

interferon glycoproteins released from cells infected with a virus, which restrict, or *interfere* with, the growth of viruses, and they limit the growth of cells, hence their use in cancer treatment (which is as yet of indeterminate value). There are three human interferons: (1) from white blood cells; (2) from connective tissue; and (3) from lymphocytes (*see* interleukins). Sufficient quantities of interferon can now be produced by genetic engineering.

interleukin one of several cytokines (molecules secreted by a cell to regulate other cells nearby, e.g. *see* interferon) that act between leucocytes. There are eight interleukins currently recognized, and some are involved in functions such as the recognition of antigens, enhancing the action of macrophages and the production of other cytokines, e.g. interleukin-2 promotes the production of g-interferon and is used in the treatment of melanoma.

intestinal flora the bacteria usually found in the intestine, some of which synthesize vitamin K. An acidic surrounding is produced by the bacteria and this helps lessen infection by pathogens unable to withstand the acidic conditions.

intestine the part of the alimentary canal or tract between stomach and anus where final digestion and absorption of food matter occur in addition to the absorption of water and production of faeces. The intestine is divided into the small intestine comprising duodenum, ileum and jejunum, and the large intestine made up of the caecum, vermiform appendix, colon and rectum. The length of the intestine in man is about 30 feet.

intolerance when a patient is unable to metabolize a drug. There is usually an associated adverse reaction.

intrinsic factor this term refers to a substance that is produced by the membrane lining the stomach and that is essential for the absorption of vitamin B_{12} (cyanocobalamin) from the intestines. Deficiency of vitamin B_{12} may be caused by a lack of the vitamin itself or a lack of the intrinsic factor, either of which results in pernicious anaemia.

invasion when bacteria enter the body; but more commonly used to describe the process whereby malignant cancer cells move into nearby normal and deeper tissues and gain access to the blood vessels.

isomers these are molecules that have the same molecular weight and chemical formula but have different physical structures and so different properties.

jejunum the part of the small intestine lying before the ileum and after the duodenum. Its main function is the absorption of digested food and its lining has numerous finger-like projections (villi) that increase the surface area for absorption.

joints connections between bones (and cartilages). Joints can be divided upon their structure and the degree to which they permit movement. *Fibrous* joints are fixed by fibrous tissue binding bones together, e.g. the bones of the skull. *Cartilaginous* joints are slightly movable. These have discs of cartilage between bones so that only limited movement is permitted over one joint but over several adjacent joints, considerable flexure is achieved, as with the spine. The final category is *synovial* joints, which can move freely. Each synovial joint comprises the bones, cartilage over the ends, then a *capsule* (sheath of fibrous tissue) from which the ligaments form, and a synovial membrane with synovial fluid to lubricate the joint.

This type of joint then occurs in two forms: hinge joints allowing planar movement (e.g. the knee) and ball and socket joints permitting all-round movement (e.g. the hip). Joints are subject to various conditions and diseases, which may be linked to the action of free radicals and insufficient levels of certain vitamins in the body.

keratomalacia this disease results from severe deficiency of vitamin A. It develops from night-blindness, red and swollen eyelids, photophobia and dry, rough, painful conjunctival tissues. Later symptoms include a dull, hazy cornea of the eye, which will ulcerate and develop holes, leading to blindness if no treatment is given. The condition is very serious.

Korsakoff's syndrome a neurological disorder described by the Russian neuropsychiatrist Sergei Korsakoff (1854–1900) characterized by short-term memory loss, disorientation and confabulation (the invention and detailed description of events, situations and experiences to cover gaps in the memory). The condition is caused primarily by alcoholism and a deficiency of thiamine (vital in converting carbohydrate to glucose).

Kreb's Cycle a complex cycle by which acetyl co-enzyme A is broken down, in the presence of oxygen, to produce energy in the form of ATP (adenosine triphosphate). The acetyl co-enzyme A or acetate, which is used in the process, is derived from carbohydrates, fats or proteins that were oxidized during glycolysis. The process makes hydrogen atoms or electrons available to the electron transport chain, and that allows ATP to be produced. It occurs in the mitochondria, which are found in all animal cells. The Kreb's Cycle both produces energy and forms chemicals that are required to form many cell components.

lesion a wound or injury to body tissues. Also an area of tissue, which, because of damage caused by disease or wounding, does not function fully. Thus primary lesions include tumours and ulcers, and from primary lesions secondaries may form.

leucocyte (*or* **leukocyte**) a white blood cell, so called because it contains no haemoglobin. It also differs from red blood cells in having a nucleus. Leucocytes are formed in the bone marrow, spleen, thymus and lymph nodes, and there are three types: granulocytes, comprising 70 per cent of all white blood cells, lymphocytes (25 per cent) and monocytes (5 per cent). Granulocytes help combat bacterial and viral infection and may be involved in allergies. Lymphocytes destroy foreign bodies either directly or through production of antibodies and monocytes ingest bacteria and foreign bodies by the process called *phagocytosis* (engulfing microorganisms and cell debris to remove them from the body). In disease, immature forms of leucocytes may appear in the blood (ultimately forming both red and white blood cells).

leukotrienes a group of biologically active compounds that occur naturally in leucocytes (white blood cells). The compounds are derived from arachadonic acid, an essential fatty acid produced in the body from linolenic acid. Leukotrienes probably take part in allergic or inflammatory reactions and may play a role in the development of allergic diseases such as arthritis and rheumatoid arthritis.

linkage two or more genes are said to be linked together if they occur close to each other on the same chromosome. The genes are thus likely to be inherited together as will be characteristics that they represent. This is because the linked genes are more likely to be together in nuclei formed as a result of meiosis (the chromosomal division that produces the gametes).

lipoprotein a group of conjugated proteins where lipids play an integral part of the structure. They are made in the liver and are important in the transport of lipids in the blood and lymph fluids. Lipoproteins also move lipids from the liver to the site of fat deposition.

liver a very important organ of the body, with many functions critical in regulating metabolic processes. It is also the largest gland in the body, weighing around 1.5kg. It occupies the top right-hand part of the abdominal cavity and is made up of four lobes. It is fastened to the abdominal wall by ligaments and sits beneath the diaphragm, and upon the right kidney, large intestine, duodenum and stomach.

There are two blood vessels supplying the liver: the hepatic artery delivers oxygenated blood, while the hepatic portal vein conveys digested food from the stomach. Among its functions, the liver converts excess glucose to glycogen for storage as a food reserve; excess amounts of amino acids are converted to urea for excretion by the kidneys; bile is produced for storage in the gall bladder and lipolysis occurs; some poisons are broken down (detoxified) hence the beneficial effect of the hepatic portal vein carrying blood to the liver rather than it going around the body first.

The liver also synthesizes blood-clotting substances such as fibrinogen and prothrombin and the anticoagulant heparin; it breaks down red blood cells at the end of their life and processes the haemoglobin for iron, which is stored; vitamin A is synthesized and stored and it also stores vitamins B_{12}, D, E and K. In the embryo it forms red blood cells. Such is the chemical and biochemical activity of the liver that significant heat energy is generated and this organ is a major contributor of heat to the body.

lordosis this is the inward curvature of the spine. It is normal up to a point but can become exaggerated by faulty posture in adolescence or because of disease affecting the vertebrae and the spinal muscles, e.g. Duchenne's muscular dystrophy.

lower reference nutrient intake (LRNI) the nutrient requirements for people with lower needs. This would not be enough for most people to avoid deficiency problems.

lymph a colourless, watery fluid that surrounds the body tissues and circulates in the lymphatic system. Derived from blood and similar to plasma, it is comprised of 95 per cent water, with protein, sugar, salts and lymphocytes. The lymph is circulated by muscular action, and it passes through lymph nodes, which act as filters, and is eventually returned to the blood via the thoracic duct (one of the two main vessels of the lymphatic system).

lymphatic system the network of vessels, valves, nodes, etc, that carry lymph from the tissues to the bloodstream and help maintain the internal fluid environment of the body. Lymph drains into capillaries and larger vessels, passing through nodes and going eventually into two large vessels (the thoracic duct and right lymphatic duct), which return it to the bloodstream by means of the innominate veins.

lymphocyte a type of white blood cell (leucocyte) produced in the bone marrow and also present in the spleen, thymus gland and lymph nodes, which forms a vital component of the immune system. There are two types: B-cells and T-cells. B-cells produce antibodies and search out and bind with particular antigens. T-cells circulate through the thymus gland where they differentiate. When they contact an antigen, large numbers of T-cells are generated, which secrete chemical compounds to assist the B-cells in destroying, e.g. bacteria.

lysis the destruction of cells or tissues because of breakdown of the cell membranes.

macrophage a large scavenger cell (phagocyte) that develops from monocytes. They are found in the liver, spleen, bone marrow, lymph nodes, connective tissue and the *microglia* of the central nervous system. They remove foreign bodies such as bacteria from blood and tissues. *Fixed macrophages* remain in one place in the connective tissue, *free macrophages* are able to migrate between cells and gather at sites of infection to remove bacteria and other foreign material. They move freely in the blood and lymph fluids.

malabsorption syndrome a group of diseases in which there is a reduction in the normal absorption of digested food materials in the small intestine. The food materials involved are commonly fats, vitamins, minerals, amino acids and iron. The diseases include coeliac disease, pancreatitis, cystic fibrosis, sprue and stagnant loop syndrome and also surgical removal of a part of the small intestine.

malignant name given to a condition that may become life threatening if left untreated. A term used in several ways but commonly referring to a tumour that proliferates rapidly and destroys surrounding healthy tissue, and that can spread via the lymphatic and blood system to other parts of the body. The term is also applied to a form of a disease that is more serious than the usual one and is life-threatening, such as *malignant smallpox* and malignant hypertension.

malnutrition a condition caused either by an unbalanced diet, i.e. too much of one type of food at the expense of others or by an inadequate food intake (*subnutrition*), which can lead to starvation. The condition may also arise because of internal disfunction, e.g. malabsorption or other *metabolic* disturbance within the body.

mast cell a large cell, many of which are found in loose connective tissue. The cytoplasm contains numerous granules with chemicals important in the body including histamine, serotonin, heparin and the antibody immunoglobulin E. All are important in allergic and inflammatory responses.

membrane a thin composite layer of lipoprotein surrounding an individual cell or a thin layer of tissue surrounding an organ, lining a cavity or tube or separating tissues and organs within the body.

Menke's syndrome a disorder that runs in families where there is abnormal absorption of copper from the intestines. Symptoms in adults are the growth of sparse, kinky hair while infants may show cerebral degeneration, retarded growth and early death.

metabolism the sum of all the physical and chemical changes within cells and tissues that maintain life and growth. The breakdown processes that occur are known as *catabolic* (*catabolism*), and those that build materials up are called *anabolic* (*anabolism*). The term may also be applied to describe one particular set of changes, e.g. *protein metabolism*. *Basal metabolism* is the minimum amount of energy required to maintain the body's vital processes, e.g. heartbeat and respiration, and is usually assessed by means of various measurements taken while a person is at rest.

metastasis the process by which a malignant tumour spreads to a distant part of the body, and also refers to the secondary growth that results from this. The spread is accomplished by means of three routes, the blood circulation, lymphatic system and across body cavities.

migraine a very severe throbbing headache, usually on one side of the head, which is often accompanied by disturbances in vision, nausea and vomiting. Migraine is a common condition and seems to be triggered by any one or several of a number of factors. These include anxiety, fatigue, watching television or video screens, loud noises, flickering lights (e.g. strobe lights) and certain foods such as cheese and chocolate or alcoholic drinks. The cause is unknown but thought to involve constriction followed by dilation of blood vessels in the brain and an outpouring of fluid into surrounding tissues. The attack can last up to 24 hours and treatment is by means of bed rest in a darkened, quiet room and pain-relieving drugs. Migraine may be linked to food intolerance and insufficient vitamin intake.

mitochondrion a tiny rodlike structure, numbers of which are present in the cytoplasm of every cell. *Mitochondria* contain enzymes and ATP involved in cell metabolism.

monocyte the largest type of white blood cell (leucocyte) with a kidney-shaped nucleus found in the blood and lymph. It ingests foreign bodies such as bacteria and tissue particles.

mucous membrane a moist membrane that lines many tubes and cavities within the body and is lubricated with mucus. The structure of a mucous membrane varies according to its site and they are found, for example, lining the mouth, respiratory, urinary and digestive tracts. Each has a surface epithelium, a layer containing various cells and glands that secrete mucus. Beneath this lie connective tissue and muscle layers, the *laminae propria* and *muscularis mucosa* respectively, the whole forming a pliable layer.

mucus a slimy substance secreted by mucous membranes as a lubricant, and composed mainly of glycoproteins of which the chief one is *mucin*. It is a clear viscous fluid, which may contain enzymes, and has a protective function. It is normally present in small amounts but the quantity increases if inflammation and/or infection is present. Production of mucus is affected by the action of free radicals and hence joint problems can arise.

multiple sclerosis a disease of the brain and spinal cord that affects the myelin sheaths of nerves and disrupts their function. It usually affects people below the age of 40 and its cause is unknown, but is the subject of much research. The disease is characterized by the presence of patches of hardened (sclerotic) connective tissue irregularly scattered through the brain and spinal cord. At first the fatty part of the nerve sheaths breaks down and is absorbed, leaving bare nerve fibres, and then connective tissue is laid down. Symptoms depend upon the site of the patches in the central nervous system and the disease is characterized by periods of progression and remission. However, they include unsteady gait and apparent clumsiness, tremor of the limbs, involuntary eye movements, speech disorders, bladder disfunction and paralysis. The disease can progress very slowly but generally there is a tendency for the paralysis to become more marked.

muscular dystrophy also known as *myopathy*, this is any of a group of diseases that involve wasting of muscles and in which an hereditary factor is involved. The disease is classified according to the groups of muscles that it affects and the age of the person involved. The disease usually appears in childhood and causes muscle fibres to degenerate and to be replaced by fatty and fibrous tissue. The affected muscles eventually lose all power of contraction, causing great disability, and affected children are prone to chest and other infections that may prove fatal in their weakened state. The cause of the disease is not entirely understood but the commonest form, *Duchenne muscular dystrophy*, is sex-linked and recessive. Hence it nearly always affects boys, with the mother as a carrier, and appears in very early childhood.

mutagen any substance or agent that increases the rate of mutation in body cells, examples being various chemicals, viruses and radiation. Mutagens increase the number rather than the range of mutations beyond that which might be expected.

mutation a change that takes place in the DNA (the genetic material) of the chromosomes of a cell, which is normally a rare event. The change may involve the structure or number of whole chromosomes or take place at one gene site. Mutations are caused by faulty replication of the cell's genetic material at cell division. If normal body (*somatic*) cells are involved there may be a growth of altered cells or a tumour, or these may be attacked and destroyed by the immune system. In any event, this type of mutation cannot be passed on—if the sex cells (ova or sperm) are involved in the mutation, the alteration may be passed on to the offspring producing a changed characteristic.

myasthenia gravis a serious and chronic condition of uncertain cause, which may be an auto-immune disease. It is more common among young people, especially women (men tend to be affected over 40). Rest and avoidance of unnecessary exertion is essential to conserve muscle strength as there is a reduction in the ability of the neurotransmitter, acetylcholine, to effect muscle contraction. There is a weakening that affects skeletal muscles and those for breathing and swallowing etc. However, there is little wasting of the muscles themselves. It seems the body produces antibodies that interfere with the acetylcholine receptors in the muscle, and that the thymus gland may be the original source of these receptors. Surgical removal of the thymus gland is one treatment. Other treatment is by means of drugs, e.g. Pyridodstigmine, that inhibit the activity of the enzyme *cholinesterase*, which destroys excess acetylcholine. Other *immunosuppressive* drugs are used to suppress production of the antibodies that interfere with the receptors.

myocardial infarction the death of an area of heart muscle because of lack of oxygen or because the blood supply to that area of the heart is disrupted. It occurs during a coronary thrombosis, where there is a sudden blockage of one of the coronary arteries by a blood clot or thrombus, which interrupts the blood supply to the heart. Myocardial infarction can result in the formation of free radicals when the blood flow returns to normal through the affected area. This increases the risks of a another heart attack occurring and damages the heart muscle even more.

myoglobin an iron-containing pigment that is similar to haemoglobin, and occurs in muscle cells. It binds oxygen from haemoglobin and releases it in the muscle cells.

nephrocalcinosis a condition where calcium deposits are formed in the kidneys. It can be caused by excess calcium levels in the blood, over-activity of the parathyroid glands or an abnormality in the kidney.

nervous system the complete system of tissues and cells including nerves, neurons, synapses and receptors (a special cell, sensitive to a particular stimulus, which then sends an impulse through the nervous system). The nervous system operates through the transmission of impulses that are conducted rapidly to and from muscles, organs, etc. It consists of the central nervous system (brain and spinal cord) and the peripheral nervous system that includes the cranial and spinal nerves.

neurotransmitter one of several chemical substances released in minute quantities by axon tips into the synapse to enable a nerve impulse to cross. It diffuses across the space and may depolarize the opposite membrane allowing the production of an action potential. Outside the central nervous system acetylcholine is a major neurotransmitter, and noradrenaline is released in the sympathetic nervous system. Acetylcholine and noradrenaline also operate within the central nervous system as does dopamine, amongst others.

neutrophil a type of white blood cell that is capable of ingesting and killing bacteria and is an important part of our defence against infection.

night-blindness (*or* **nyctalopia**) poor vision in dim light or at night because of a deficiency within the rod cells responsible for such vision. The cause may be a lack of vitamin A in the diet or a congenital defect.

nitrates salts of nitric acid, HNO_3. They are found in fertilizers and have the formula NO_3. Nitrate in foodstuffs can be from air pollution or agricultural fertilizers and in the body it is converted into nitrites.

nitrites salts with the $[NO_2]^-$ ion that are derived from nitrous acid, HNO_2. They are used as food preservatives in sausages and tinned meats. Nitrites are converted into nitrosamines in the intestines of humans.

nitrosamines are compounds that can be formed from nitrites in the human body. Most of the nitrosamines are carcinogenic when tested in experimental animals and are thought to damage human cells. Vitamin C acts to reduce the levels produced in the intestines.

non-Hodgkin's lymphoma this name is given to any type of malignant lymphoma that is not Hodgkin's disease. Symptoms can include an enlarged lymph node, weakness, weight loss, fever and anaemia. Disturbances to the gastrointestinal tract, enlarged liver and spleen, bone lesions and malabsorption of nutrients can develop later in the disease. Kinds of lymphoma include Burkitt's lymphoma, giant follicular lymphoma and mixed cell malignant lymphoma.

nucleic acid a linear molecule that occurs in two forms: DNA (deoxyribonucleic acid) and RNA (ribonucleic acid), composed of four nucleotides. DNA is the major part of chromosomes in the cell nucleus while RNA is found outside the nucleus and is involved in protein synthesis.

nucleotide the basic molecular building block of the nucleic acids RNA and DNA. A nucleotide comprises a five-carbon sugar molecule with a phosphate group and an organic base. The organic base can be a *purine*, e.g. adenine and guanine, or a *pyrimidine*, e.g. cytosine and thymine as in DNA. In RNA uracil replaces thymine.

nucleus the large organelle (a membrane-bounded cell constituent) that contains the DNA. Unless it is dividing a nucleolus with RNA is present. During cell division the DNA, which is normally dispersed with protein (as chromatin), forms visible chromosomes.

oedema a condition where fluid accumulates in the interstitial spaces between tissues, e.g. in the joints.

oesophagus the first part of the alimentary canal lying between the pharynx and stomach. The mucous membrane lining produces secretions to lubricate food as it passes and the movement of the food to the stomach is achieved by waves of muscular movement called *peristalsis*.

oestrogen one of a group of steroid hormones secreted mainly by the ovaries and to a lesser extent by the adrenal cortex and placenta. (The testes also produce small amounts.) Oestrogens control the female secondary sexual characteristics, i.e. enlargement of the breasts, change in the profile of the pelvic girdle, pubic hair growth and deposition of body fat. High levels are produced at ovulation and with progesterone they regulate the female reproductive cycle.

oncogene any gene directly involved in cancer, whether in viruses or in the individual.

oncogenic any factor that causes cancer. This may be an organism, a chemical or some environmental condition. Some viruses are oncogenic and have the result of making a normal cell become a cancer cell.

organic compound any compound that contains carbon in its structure.

ossification (*or* **osteogenesis**) bone formation, which occurs in several stages via special cells called osteoblasts. Collagen fibres form a network in connective tissue and then a cement of polysaccharide is laid down. Finally, calcium salts are distributed among the cement as tiny crystals. The osteoblasts are enclosed as bone cells (osteocytes).

osteoarthritis a form of arthritis involving joint cartilage with accompanying changes in the associated bone. It usually involves the loss of cartilage and the development of osteophytes at the bone margins. The function of the joint (most often the thumb, knee and hip) is affected and it becomes painful. The condition may be caused by overuse, and affects those past middle age. It also may complicate other joint diseases. Treatment usually involves administering analgesics, possibly anti-inflammatory drugs and the use of corrective or replacement surgery.

osteoblast a specialized cell responsible for the formation of bone.

osteomalacia a softening of the bones, and the adult equivalent of rickets, which is caused by a lack of vitamin D. This vitamin is obtained from the diet and is produced on exposure to sunlight, and it is necessary for the uptake of calcium from food.

osteoporosis a loss of bone tissue because of its being resorbed, resulting in bones that become brittle and likely to fracture. It is common in menopausal women and can result from long-term steroid therapy. Hormone replacement therapy is a treatment available to women, but supplementation with selected vitamins, minerals and essential fatty acids can be of considerable benefit, with fewer side effects than conventional drugs.

oxidative phosphorylation the

production of ATP (adenosine triphosphate), which is linked to the electron transport chain that takes place in the mitochondria in our cells. Reduced forms of the co-enzymes NAD (nicotinamide adenine dinucleotide) and FAD (flavin adenine nucleotide) are used to produce the high energy ATP molecule. NAD and FAD require niacin (vitamin B_3) and riboflavin (vitamin B_2) for their formation.

oxidation a process where electrons are removed from a compound and its oxidation state is increased. The oxidation state is a measure of the difference (+ve or –ve) between the number of electrons within an atom in a compound and the number of electrons in an atom of the element. For example, Sodium (Na) in sodium chloride Na^+Cl^- has a charge of 1^+. This is because it has been oxidized and lost an electron to the chloride atom. Oxidation can be the addition of oxygen to a compound, but only in organic compounds.

oxytocin a hormone from the pituitary gland that causes the uterus to contract during labour and prompts lactation because of contraction of muscle fibres in the milk ducts of the breasts.

pallor an abnormal paleness of skin because of a reduced blood flow, or a lack of the normal pigments. It may be due directly to anaemia or shock to spending an excessive amount of time indoors.

pancreas a gland with both endocrine and exocrine functions. It is located between the duodenum and spleen, behind the stomach, and is about 15cm long. There are two types of cells producing secretions, the *acini*, which produce pancreatic juice that goes to the intestine via a system of ducts. This contains an alkaline mixture of salt and enzymes—trypsin and chymotrypsin to digest proteins, amylase to break down starch and lipase to aid digestion of fats. The second cell types are in the islets of langerhans and these produce two hormones, insulin and glucagon, secreted directly into the blood for control of sugar levels.

paralytic ileus this is a decrease or complete absence of intestinal peristalsis (movement of food through the intestines). The condition can arise after abdominal surgery, fractured ribs, severe metabolic disease, myocardial infarction or heavy metal poisoning. The symptoms include abdominal tenderness, nausea, vomiting, fever, dehydration, respiratory distress and lack of bowel sounds.

paranoia an abnormal mental condition typified by delusions associated with a certain, complicated system, which usually involves feelings of persecution or grandeur. The complex web of delusion may develop with time, and with some logic, so that it may appear plausible and the person seems normal in other aspects and behaviour, save for that involving the delusions.

parasite any organism that obtains its nutrients by living in or on the body of another organism (the *host*). The extent to which the host is damaged by the parasite ranges from virtually no effect to, in extreme cases, death. Parasites in humans include worms, viruses, fungi, etc.

parenteral nutrition provision of food by any means other than by the mouth. For patients with burns, renal failure, etc, or after major surgery, this mode of feeding may be necessary and is accomplished intravenously. Protein, fat and carbohydrate can all be delivered as special solutions containing all the essential compounds. The main hazard of such a system is the risk of infection and reactions to the solutions introduced, e.g. hyperglycaemia can result.

Parkinson's disease a progressive condition occurring in mid to late life, which results in a rigidity of muscles affecting the voice and face rather than those in the limbs. A tremor also develops possibly in one hand initially and then spreading to other limbs and it appears most pronounced when sitting. The disease is usually caused by a deficiency in the neurotransmitter dopamine, because of degeneration of the basal ganglia of the brain. There is no cure available, but a number of drugs are able, to varying degrees, to control the condition.

pathogen the name given to any organism that causes disease. Human pathogens include bacteria, viruses, protozoans and parasites.

pellagra this is a nutritional deficiency disease caused either by too little niacin or tryptophan or by a defect in the metabolism, which means tryptophan cannot be converted into niacin. The disease is common in maize-eating areas as the niacin in the maize is held in a bound form that cannot be used by humans. Symptoms include scaly dermatitis, particularly on skin exposed to the sun, inflammation of the mucous membranes, loss of appetite, diarrhoea or constipation and headache. These symptoms may last about a fortnight when tremors, weakness of the legs, sleeplessness and mental disturbances can arise. The disease can recur every spring for several years, with each attack becoming more severe and the patient grows more emaciated with the mental disturbances, increasing to include depression, disorientation, confusion, delirium and hallucination. Paralysis and dementia can result in some cases, if treatment is not given.

peptide an organic compound made up of two or more amino acids and collectively named by the number of amino acids. A dipeptide therefore contains two, and a polypeptide many.

pernicious anaemia a type of anaemia caused by vitamin B_{12} deficiency, which results from dietary lack or the failure to produce the substance that enables B_{12} to be absorbed from the bowel. This in turn results in a lack of red blood cell production and megaloblasts in the bone marrow. The condition is easily treated by regular injections of the vitamin, which continue throughout the patient's lifetime.

phagocyte a cell that can ingest and digest pathogens including bacteria, viruses, protozoa, fungi, cell debris and other small particles. The group includes the neutrophils and the macrophages of the white blood cells.

platelets these are the smallest cells in the blood and are typically 1–2mm in diameter. They are disc-shaped, contain no haemoglobin and have several functions, all of which relate to the coagulation of blood.

polycythaemia this is a disease where there is an increase in the haemoglobin content of the blood and hence an increase in the number of red blood cells. There is normally an associated increase in the numbers of white blood cells and platelets. Symptoms may include headache, blood clots, itching, bluish discoloration of the skin and mucous membranes and excess blood levels. The disease can happen as a result of respiratory, heart or circulatory diseases and is an adaptation of the human body to the low oxygen levels found at high altitudes. It can be treated by blood letting or by the use of cytotoxic drugs or radiotherapy to kill and remove some blood cells.

precancerous any condition that is not malignant but is known will become so if left untreated.

premenstrual tension (*or* **syndrome**) the occurrence for up to ten days before menstruation, of such symptoms as headache, nervousness and irritability, emotional disturbance, depression, fatigue with other physical manifestations such as swelling of legs and breasts, and constipation. The condition usually disappears soon after menstruation begins. The cause is not known although the hormone progesterone is probably involved in some way. Supplements of vitamin B_6 and gamma-linolenic acid may help ease the condition.

prophylactic treatment this is an action that is designed to prevent a disease from occurring or to prevent a mild complaint from becoming more severe. It can be a biological (e.g. vaccine), chemical (e.g. drug) or mechanical agent, which destroys or prevents the entry of infectious organisms into the body. In terms of diet and nutrients, prophylactic treatment generally means taking certain vitamins or minerals in doses that are higher than the RDA values to prevent the development of diseases such as arteriosclerosis, heart disease or cancer. These vitamins and minerals may boost the immune system or increase the levels of naturally protective antioxidants in our blood, and so reduce the damage caused by harmful chemicals and free radicals to our cells.

prostaglandin (PG) a group of compounds derived from essential fatty acids that act in a way that is similar to hormones. They are found in most body tissues (but especially semen) where they are released as local regulators (in the uterus, brain, lungs, etc). A number have been identified, two of which act antagonistically on blood vessels, PGE causing dilation, PGF constriction. Certain prostaglandins cause uterine contraction in labour, and others are involved in the body's defence mechanisms.

prosthetic group these are non-protein molecules that combine with a protein to form a more complex molecule. Many important enzymes in the metabolism require co-enzymes to act as prosthetic groups so they can function effectively.

protein a large group of organic compounds containing carbon, hydrogen, oxygen, sulphur and nitrogen, with individual molecules built up of amino acids in long polypeptide chains. Globular protein includes enzymes, antibodies, carrier proteins (e.g. haemoglobin) some hormones, etc. Fibrous proteins have elasticity and strength and are found in muscle, connective tissue and also chromosomes.

Proteins are thus vital to the body and are synthesized from their constituent amino acids, which are obtained from digestion of dietary protein.

prothrombin this is a protein found in the blood plasma, which is the precursor of thrombin. It is a glycoprotein made up of two peptide chains and is synthesized in the liver using vitamin K. When exposed to calcium and thromboplastin, thrombin is formed and this is the first step in blood clotting.

psoriasis a chronic skin disease the cause of which is unknown and the treatment of which is palliative. The affected skin appears as itchy, scaly red areas, starting usually around the elbows and knees. It often runs in families and may be associated with anxiety, commencing usually in childhood or adolescence. Treatment involves the use of ointments and creams with some drugs and vitamin A.

purine this is a chemical group with a two-ring molecular structure that contains nitrogen. The most common purines are adenine and guanine, which are the nucleotides found in DNA and ribonucleic acids. Purines are also found in some co-enzymes. Purines are present in many drugs including some diuretics, muscle relaxants, myocardial stimulants and caffeine.

purpura this disorder takes the form of a purple skin rash caused by bleeding into the skin from blood capillaries. Purpura can develop because of defects in the capillaries or because of a lack of blood platelets. Symptoms may include feverishness, lassitude and the characteristic red/purple spots. These spots can progress from purple to nearly black, then green and yellow in colour in the same way as a bruise progresses. Several crops of the rash can appear over a period of time. This disease can be part of the symptoms of scurvy, which results from severe deficiency of vitamin C.

pyrimidine a group of nitrogen-containing, single-ring molecules that include cytosine, thymine and uracil. These three pyrimidines are the nucleotides found in DNA and ribonucleic acid (RNA). Pyrimidines and purines compose all the nucleotides found in both DNA and RNA.

radiotherapy the therapeutic use of penetrating radiation including X-rays, beta rays and gamma rays. These may be derived from X-ray machines or radioactive isotopes and are especially employed in the treatment of cancer. The main disadvantages of radiotherapy is that there may be damage to normal, healthy surrounding tissues.

RDA recommended dietary allowance, the daily intake of protein, carbohydrate, vitamin or mineral that is required to prevent nutrient deficiencies. Some people believe this value is too low to ensure good health in all people as it only applies to healthy persons and excludes babies, pregnant and nursing mothers, people over 50, people with chronic or infectious diseases, people with metabolic disorders, smokers and people on permanent medication. These people typically require more vitamins.

red blood cell (*or* **erythrocyte**) made in the bone marrow and occurs as a red disc, concave on both sides, full of haemoglobin. These cells are responsible for carrying oxygen to tissues and carbon dioxide away. The latter is removed in the form of the bicarbonate ion (HCO_3^-), in exchange for a chloride ion (Cl^-). There are approximately five million erythrocytes in one millilitre of blood and they are active for about 120 days before being absorbed by macrophages.

reduction a process where one or more electrons is added to a molecule or atom. The charge on an ion in a molecule is decreased and made more negative. In organic chemistry, reduction can mean the addition of hydrogen or the removal of oxygen from a compound.

reference nutrient intake (RNI) this is similar to the RDA and is a value for vitamins and minerals that is higher than the needs of most of the population.

reperfusion injury this is a type of damage that is done to cells when the blood supply returns to an area that has been deprived of oxygen. When reperfusion occurs, several biochemical reactions lead to large quantities of oxygen radicals being produced. These radicals damage the cells of the heart muscle, intestines, arteries and the brain. The free radicals react with polyunsaturated fatty acids in the cells to form aldehydes and lipoxins, which are toxic to the cells.

resistance the degree of natural immunity that an individual possesses against a certain disease or diseases. The term is also applied to the degree with which a disease or disease-causing organism can withstand treatment with drugs such as a course of antibiotics.

respiration the whole process by which air is drawn into and out of the lungs during which oxygen is absorbed into the bloodstream and carbon dioxide and water are given off. *External respiration* is the actual process of breathing and the exchange of gases that takes place in the lungs. *Internal respiration* is the process by which oxygen is given up from the blood circulation to the tissues, in all parts of the body, and carbon dioxide is taken up to be transported back to the lungs and eliminated.

The process of drawing air into the lungs is known as *inhalation* or *inspiration* and expelling it out as *exhalation* or *expiration*. The rate at which this occurs is known as the *respiratory rate* and it is about 18 times a minute in a static healthy adult.

rheumatism a general term used to describe aches and pains in joints and muscles.

rheumatoid arthritis the second most common form of joint disease after osteoarthritis, which usually affects the feet, ankles, fingers and wrists. The condition is diagnosed by means of X-rays, which show a typical pattern of changes around the inflamed joints, known as *rheumatoid erosions*. At first there is swelling of the joint and inflammation of the synovial membrane (the membraneous sac that surrounds the joint), followed by erosion and loss of cartilage and bone. In addition, a blood test reveals the presence of *serum rheumatoid factor antibody*, which is characteristic of this condition. The condition varies greatly in its degree of severity, but at its worst can be progressive and seriously disabling. In other people, after an initial active phase, there may be a long period of remission.

A number of different drugs are used to treat the disease including analgesics and anti-inflammatory agents. Supplementation with some vitamins and minerals, e.g. Vitamin B_9, folic acid, can help ease the pain and discomfort of this condition.

ribosomes these are organelles found in the cytoplasm of cells, which are composed of ribonucleic acid and protein. They may be free in the cell or attached to a network called the endoplasmic reticulum. The ribosomes interact with types of RNA called messenger RNA and transfer RNA to assemble amino acids into a polypeptide chain. The protein is made by following the sequence of nucleotides in the RNA.

ribonucleic acid (RNA) this is a nucleic acid that acts as the genetic material for some viruses. In humans, it acts as an intermediate between DNA and protein synthesis. The RNA molecule exists as a single strand of nucleotides, linked to the ribose sugar that replaces the deoxyribose sugar found in DNA. The nucleotides found in RNA are adenine, guanine, cytosine and aracil, which replaces thymine, which is found in DNA only.

rickets this is a disease affecting children, which involves a deficiency of vitamin D. Vitamin D can be manufactured in the skin in the presence of sunlight, but dietary sources are important, especially where sunlight is lacking. The disease is characterized by soft bones that bend out of shape and cause deformities.

Bones are hardened by the deposition of calcium salts and this cannot happen in the absence of vitamin D. Treatment consists of giving vitamin D, usually in the form of calciferol, and ensuring that there is an adequate amount in the child's future diet. Vitamin D deficiency in adults causes the condition called osteomalacia.

RNA (ribonucleic acid) is a complex nucleic acid present mainly in the cytoplasm of cells but also in the nucleus. It is involved in the production of proteins and exists in three forms, ribosomal (r), transfer (t) and messenger (m) RNA. In some viruses it forms the genetic material.

rod one of the two types of light sensitive cell present in the retina of the eye. The rods enable vision in dim light because of a pigment called *rhodopsin* (*visual purple*). This pigment degenerates or bleaches when light is present and regenerates during darkness. In bright light all the pigment bleaches and the rods cannot function. Bleaching of the pigment gives rise to nerve impulses that are sent to the brain and interpreted.

roughage dietary fibre, which is necessary to maintain the healthy functioning of the bowels and helps to prevent constipation and diverticulosis. The eating of sufficient dietary fibre is thought to be important in the prevention of cancer of the colon.

saliva an alkaline liquid present in the mouth to keep the mouth moist, aid swallowing of food and through the presence of amylase enzymes to digest starch. It is secreted by the salivary glands and in addition to ptyalin, contains water, mucus and buffers (to minimize changes in acidity).

salivary glands three pairs of glands; parotid, submandibular and sublingual, that produce saliva. The stimulus to produce saliva can be the taste, smell, sight or even thought of food.

sclerosis hardening of tissue, usually after inflammation leading to parts of organs being hard and of no use. It is applied commonly to such changes in the nervous system (multiple sclerosis); in other organs it is termed fibrosis or cirrhosis.

scurvy a deficiency disease caused by a lack of vitamin C (ascorbic acid) resulting from a dietary lack of fruit and vegetables. Symptoms begin with swollen, bleeding gums and then subcutaneous bleeding, bleeding into joints, ulcers, anaemia and then fainting, diarrhoea and trouble with major organs. Untreated, it is fatal, but nowadays it is easily prevented, or cured should it arise, through correct diet or administration of the vitamin.

senile dementia an organic mental disorder of the elderly involving generalized atrophy of the brain. The result is a gradual deterioration with loss of memory, impaired judgement, confusion, emotional outbursts and irritability. The degree of the condition may vary considerably.

sex chromosomes chromosomes that play a major role in determining the sex of the bearer. Sex chromosomes contain genes that control the characteristics of the individual, e.g. testes in males, ovaries in females. Women have two X chromosomes while men have one X and one Y chromosome.

side effect the additional and unwanted effect(s) of a drug above the intended action. Sometimes side effects are harmful and may be stronger than anticipated results of the drug, or something quite different.

spina bifida a congenital malformation in newborn babies in which part of the spinal cord is exposed by a gap in the backbone. Many cases are also affected with hydrocephalus. The symptoms usually include paralysis, incontinence, a high risk of meningitis and mental retardation. There is usually an abnormally high level of alpha fetoprotein in the amniotic fluid and since this can be diagnosed and then confirmed by amniocentesis, it may be advisable to terminate these pregnancies. This condition may develop because of a deficiency of Vitamin B_9, folic acid, both before and after conception of the foetus. Supplements of folic acid are now recommended before conception and in the first few months of pregnancy.

spleen a roughly ovoid organ, coloured a deep purple, which is situated on the left of the body, behind and below the stomach. It is surrounded by a peritoneal membrane and contains a mass of lymphoid tissue. Macrophages in the spleen destroy microorganisms by phagocytosis.

The spleen produces lymphocytes, leucocytes, plasma cells and blood platelets. It also stores red blood cells for use in emergencies. Release of red blood cells is facilitated by smooth muscle under the control of the sympathetic nervous system, and when this occurs, the familiar pain called *stitch* may be experienced. The spleen removes worn out red blood cells, conserving the iron for further production in the bone marrow. Although the spleen performs many functions, it can be removed without detriment and as a result there is an increase in size of the lymphatic glands.

stenosis the abnormal narrowing of a blood vessel, heart valve or similar structure.

steroid one of a group of compounds resembling cholesterol, that are made up of four carbon rings fused together. The group includes the sterols (e.g. cholesterol), bile acids, some hormones, and vitamin D. Synthetic versions act like steroid hormones and include derivatives of the glucocorticoids used as anti-inflammatory agents for rheumatoid arthritis; oral contraceptives, usually oestrogen and progesterone derivatives; anabolic steroids such as testosterone used to treat osteoporosis and wasting.

stomach an expansion of the alimentary canal that lies between the oesophagus and the duodenum. It has thick walls of smooth muscle that contract to manipulate the food, and its exits are controlled by sphincters, the cardiac anteriorly and the pyloric at the junction with the duodenum. Mucosal cells in the lining secrete gastric juice. The food is reduced to an acidic semi-liquid, which is moved on to the duodenum.

The stomach varies in size but its greatest length is roughly 30cm and the breadth 10 or 12cm. Its capacity is approximately 1 to 1.5 litres.

stroke (*or* **apoplexy**) the physical effects, involving some form of paralysis, that result from an interruption to the brain's blood supply. The effect in the brain is secondary and the cause lies in the heart or blood vessels and may be a thrombosis, embolus, or haemorrhage. The severity of a stroke varies greatly from a temporary weakness in a limb, or tingling, to paralysis, coma and death.

sulphonamide one of a group of drugs containing the chemical group $-SO_2NH_2$. These drugs do not kill bacteria, but prevent bacterial growth and are thus very useful in controlling infections. Some side effects may occur but in general these are outweighed by the benefits.

superoxide dismutase (SOD) this is an important enzyme that has antioxidant properties in the human body. It works in either a copper-zinc form (Cu-Zn SOD) or with manganese (MnSOD) and attempts to neutralize free radicals so they cannot cause cell damage. It is the fifth most common protein in the human body and has limited use in treating some diseases of the joints.

susceptibility when there is a lack of resistance to disease, due either to poor general health, or a deficiency in defence mechanism because of another condition, e.g. AIDS. Susceptibility can be decreased by vaccination, etc.

symptom any evidence of a disease or disorder.

syndrome a number of symptoms and signs that together constitute a particular condition.

systemic lupus erythematosus (SLE) this is a chronic inflammatory disease of unknown origin. It may be triggered by exposure to sunlight, a virus, certain drugs or an infection. The disease is four times as common in women as in men, and may start as arthritis with fatigue, weight loss, weakness and a reddened rash over the nose and cheeks. Later the skin lesions may spread to the mucous membranes, the neck and other tissues. Fever, hair loss and photosensitivity may develop. Various organs can be affected but it is mainly the spleen and kidneys that degenerate causing anaemia and peritonitis among other symptoms. Unless treated with corticosteroids, renal failure and neurological problems can occur. Some people with SLE have found beneficial effects when treated with supplements of vitamins, minerals and essential fatty acids.

tamoxifen a drug used in the treatment of certain breast cancers.

temperature (of the body) the normal body temperature is around 37°C (98.4°F) but it varies considerably both between individuals and in one person throughout the day. In addition, temperature differences occur between various areas of the body being lower in the skin than internally.

therapy the treatment of disease.

thrombin an enzyme derived from prothrombin, its inactive precursor, which is formed and is active during the final stages of blood clotting (*see* coagulation).

thrombosis the process of clotting within a blood vessel producing a thrombus. It may occur within an artery or vein, often one that is diseased or damaged, and can be very serious or even fatal, e.g. stroke, coronary thrombosis.

thrombus a blood clot within a vessel that partially or totally obstructs the circulation.

thymus a gland, divided into two lobes, that is present in the neck and forms a vital part of the immune system. It is especially large in children and important in the development of the immune response and the production of lymphoid tissue. After puberty, the thymus gradually begins to shrink. Bone marrow cells, known as *stem cells*, undergo maturation within the thymus and one group, the *T-lymphocytes*, are dependent upon the gland. These are very important cells in the body, which produce antibodies.

thyroid gland a bi-lobed endocrine gland situated at the base and front of the neck. It is enclosed by fibrous tissue and well supplied with blood, and internally consists of numerous vesicles containing a jellylike colloidal substance. These vesicles produce thyroid hormone, which is rich in iodine, under the control of *thyroid stimulating hormone* released from the pituitary gland. Two hormones are produced by the gland, thyroxine and triiodothyronine, which are essential for the regulation of metabolism and growth.

thyroxine an important hormone produced by the thyroid gland and used medically to treat conditions resulting from under-activity of this gland.

tonsils usually refers to the two small masses of lymphoid tissue situated on either side at the back of the mouth (the *palatine tonsils*). However, another pair occur below the tongue, which are the *lingual tonsils* while the adenoids are the pharyngeal tonsils. All are part of the body's protective mechanism against infection.

toxin a poison produced by bacteria and by many species of plant and also present in snake venom. In the body, a toxin acts as an antigen and provokes the production of special antibodies called antitoxins. The antitoxins produced may be used in immunization to protect against the disease as with tetanus and diphtheria. An *endotoxin* is contained within the bacterial cell and only released when the organism dies and decays.

triglycerides fats consisting of three fatty acid molecules combined with glycerol, which are the form in which the body stores fat. Triglycerides are derived from the digestion of fats in food.

trypsin an important enzyme involved in the digestion of proteins. Its inactive precursor, trypsinogen, is secreted by the pancreas and converted to trypsin in the duodenum by the action of another enzyme called enteropeptidase.

tumour any abnormal swelling, occurring in any part of the body, which consists of an unusual growth of tissue and which may be malignant or benign. Tumours tend to be classified according to the tissue of which they are composed, e.g. fibroma (mainly fibrous tissue) and myoma (largely muscle fibres).

urine the body's fluid waste excreted by the kidneys. The waste products include urea, uric acid and creatinine (produced by muscles) with salt, phosphates and sulphates and ammonia also present. In a solution with about 95–96 per cent water, there may be 100 or more compounds but the vast majority occur only in trace amounts. Many diseases alter the quantity and composition of urine and its analysis is standard procedure to assist diagnosis of diseases.

urticaria (*or* **nettle rash**) an allergic reaction by an individual to some substance to which they are hypersensitive, in which the allergic response is manifested on the skin. Raised red patches develop, which may last for hours or days. There is intense itching.

The sensitivity may be to certain foods, e.g. shellfish, and the effect may occur anywhere on the body but commonly erupts on the face and trunk. If it also affects the tongue or throat, there is danger of a blockage of the airway, which would need urgent attention.

vaccination the production of immunity to a disease by inoculation with a vaccine or a specially prepared material that stimulates the production of antibodies. It was used initially to refer only to cowpox virus (which also protected against smallpox) but now is synonymous with inoculation, in immunizing against disease.

vaccine a modified preparation of a bacterium or virus that is no longer dangerous but will stimulate development of antibodies and therefore confer immunity against actual infection with the disease. Other vaccines consist of specific toxins (e.g. tetanus), or dead bacteria (e.g. cholera and typhoid). Live but weakened organisms are used against smallpox and tuberculosis.

vein one of the numerous blood vessels carrying deoxygenated blood to the right atrium of the heart (the one exception is the pulmonary vein). Each vein has three tissue layers, similar to the layers of the heart. Veins are less elastic than arteries and collapse when cut. They also contain valves to prevent back-flow.

vessel any tube that carries fluid, particularly blood or lymph.

virus the smallest microbe that is completely parasitic, because it is only capable of replication within the cells of its host. Viruses infect animals, plants and microorganisms. Viruses are classified according to their nucleic acids and can contain double or single-stranded DNA or RNA. In an infection the virus binds to the host cells and then penetrates the cell membrane to release the viral DNA or RNA, which controls the cell's metabolism to replicate itself and form new viruses. Viruses cause many diseases including influenza (single-stranded RNA), herpes (double-stranded DNA), AIDS (a retrovirus, single-stranded RNA) and also mumps, chickenpox and polio.

vitamin any of a group of organic compounds required in very small amounts in the diet to maintain good health. Deficiencies lead to specific diseases. Vitamins are divided into two groups: vitamins A, D, E and K are fat-soluble while C and B are water soluble.

Wilson's disease an inherited disease caused by a defect in the copper metabolism. The person lacks ceruloplasmin, which usually forms a complex with copper in the blood. The free copper accumulates in the liver, causing jaundice and cirrhosis, the kidneys and in the brain, causing mental retardation and symptoms similar to Parkinson's disease. If the excess copper is eliminated from the body using drugs such as penicillamine or dimercapnol, then both mental and physical development may progress as normal.

xerophthalmia a progressive disease that affects the eyes and occurs because of insufficient vitamin A intake. The cornea of the eye becomes dry and lustreless, then thickened and wrinkled. The condition is associated with night blindness and can progress to keratomalacia and possibly blindness.

X-rays the part of the electromagnetic spectrum with waves of wavelength 10^{-12} to 10^{-9}m and frequencies of 10^{17} to 10^{21}Hz. They are produced when high velocity electrons strike a target.

The rays penetrate solids to a depth that depends upon the density of the solid. X-rays of certain wavelengths will penetrate flesh but not bone. They are therefore useful in therapy and diagnosis within medicine.

Y chromosome the small chromosome that carries a dominant gene conferring maleness. Normal males have 22 matched chromosome pairs and one unmatched pair comprising one X and one Y chromosome.

During sexual reproduction the mother contributes an X chromosome, but the father contributes an X or Y chromosome, XX produces a female offspring, XY male.